BAKUGAN
BATTLE BRAWLERS
™

the battle begins!

ADAPTED BY Elizabeth Hurchalla
ADAPTATION DESIGNED AND LETTERED BY
Tomás Montalvo-Lagos

Ballantine Books * New York

A Del Rey Trade Paperback Original

Bakugan Battle Brawlers: The Battle Begins!
copyright © 2008 by Spin Master Ltd/Sega Toys.

BAKUGAN and BATTLE BRAWLERS, and all related titles, logos,
and characters are trademarks of
Spin Master LTD.
NELVANA is a trademark of Nelvana Limited.
CORUS is a trademark of Corus Entertainment Inc.
Used under license by Random House, Inc.
All Rights Reserved

CARTOON NETWORK and the logo are trademarks
of and © Cartoon Network.

Published in the United States by Del Rey, an imprint of The
Random House Publishing Group, a division of Random House,
Inc., New York.

DEL REY is a registered trademark and the Del Rey colophon is
a trademark of Random House, Inc.

ISBN 978-0-345-51368-7

Printed in the United States of America

www.delreymanga.com

9 8 7 6 5 4 3 2

Adapting editor: Elizabeth Hurchalla
Contributing editor: Jay Brown
Graphic design and lettering: Tomás Montalvo-Lagos

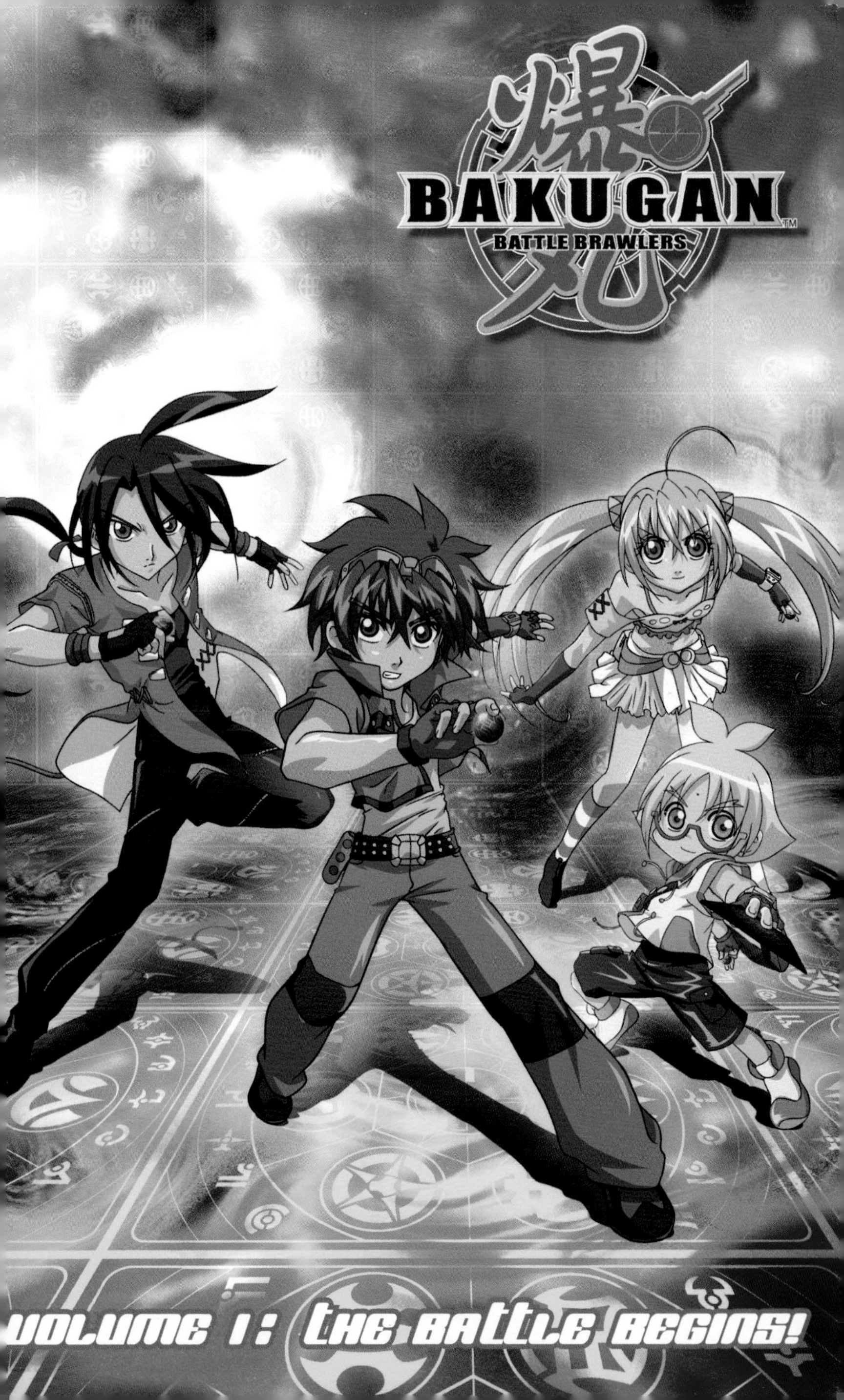
BAKUGAN™
BATTLE BRAWLERS
VOLUME 1: THE BATTLE BEGINS!

contents

CHARACTERS....................5

INTRODUCTION...................12

THE BATTLE BEGINS!.........18

THE CAST OF BAKUGAN BATTLE BRAWLERS

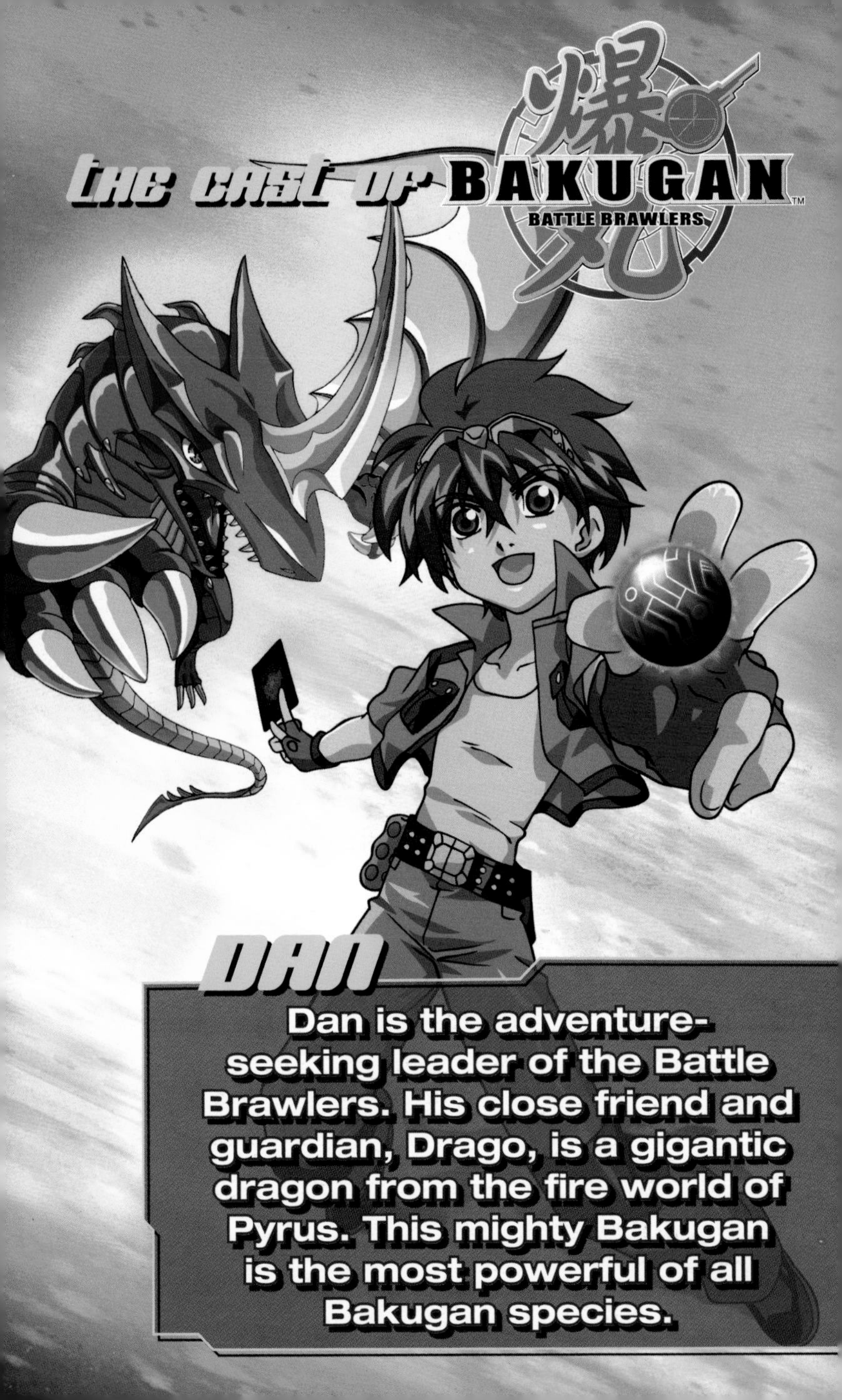

DAN

Dan is the adventure-seeking leader of the Battle Brawlers. His close friend and guardian, Drago, is a gigantic dragon from the fire world of Pyrus. This mighty Bakugan is the most powerful of all Bakugan species.

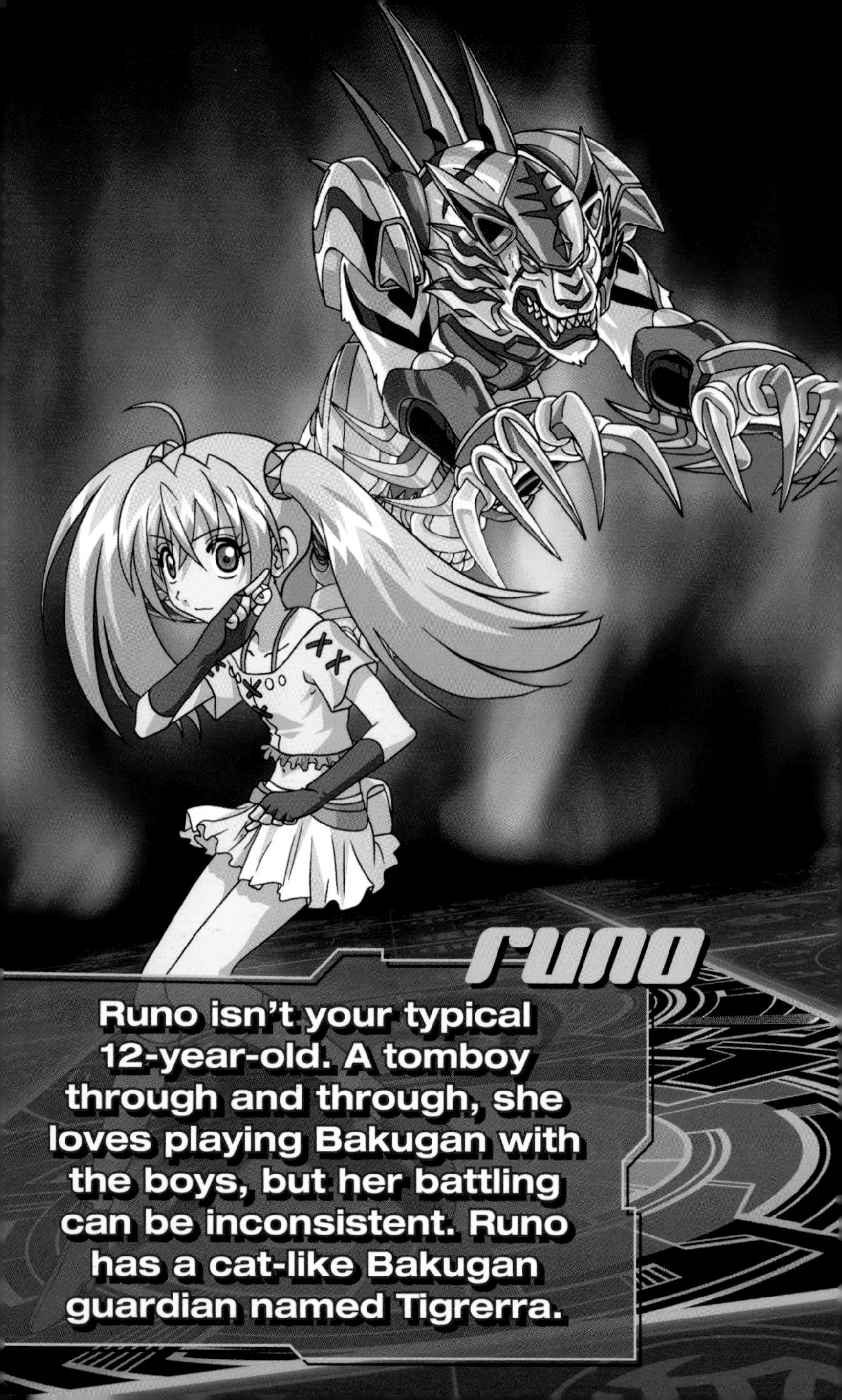

RUNO

Runo isn't your typical 12-year-old. A tomboy through and through, she loves playing Bakugan with the boys, but her battling can be inconsistent. Runo has a cat-like Bakugan guardian named Tigrerra.

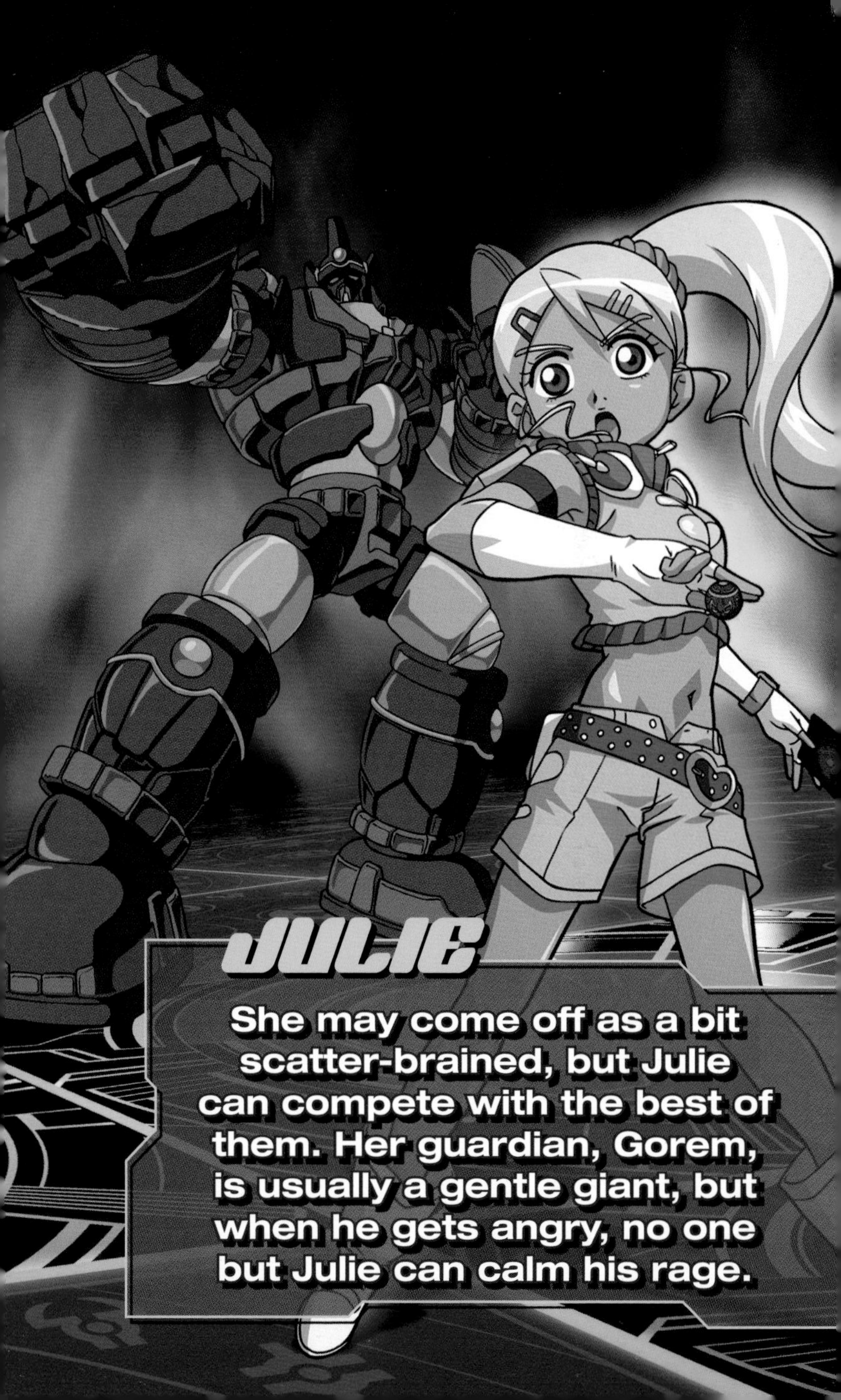
JULIE
She may come off as a bit scatter-brained, but Julie can compete with the best of them. Her guardian, Gorem, is usually a gentle giant, but when he gets angry, no one but Julie can calm his rage.

Wise beyond his years, Marucho is constantly studying the strategy behind Bakugan battles. His guardian, Preyas, may look menacing, but he has a very quirky sense of humor.

MARUCHO

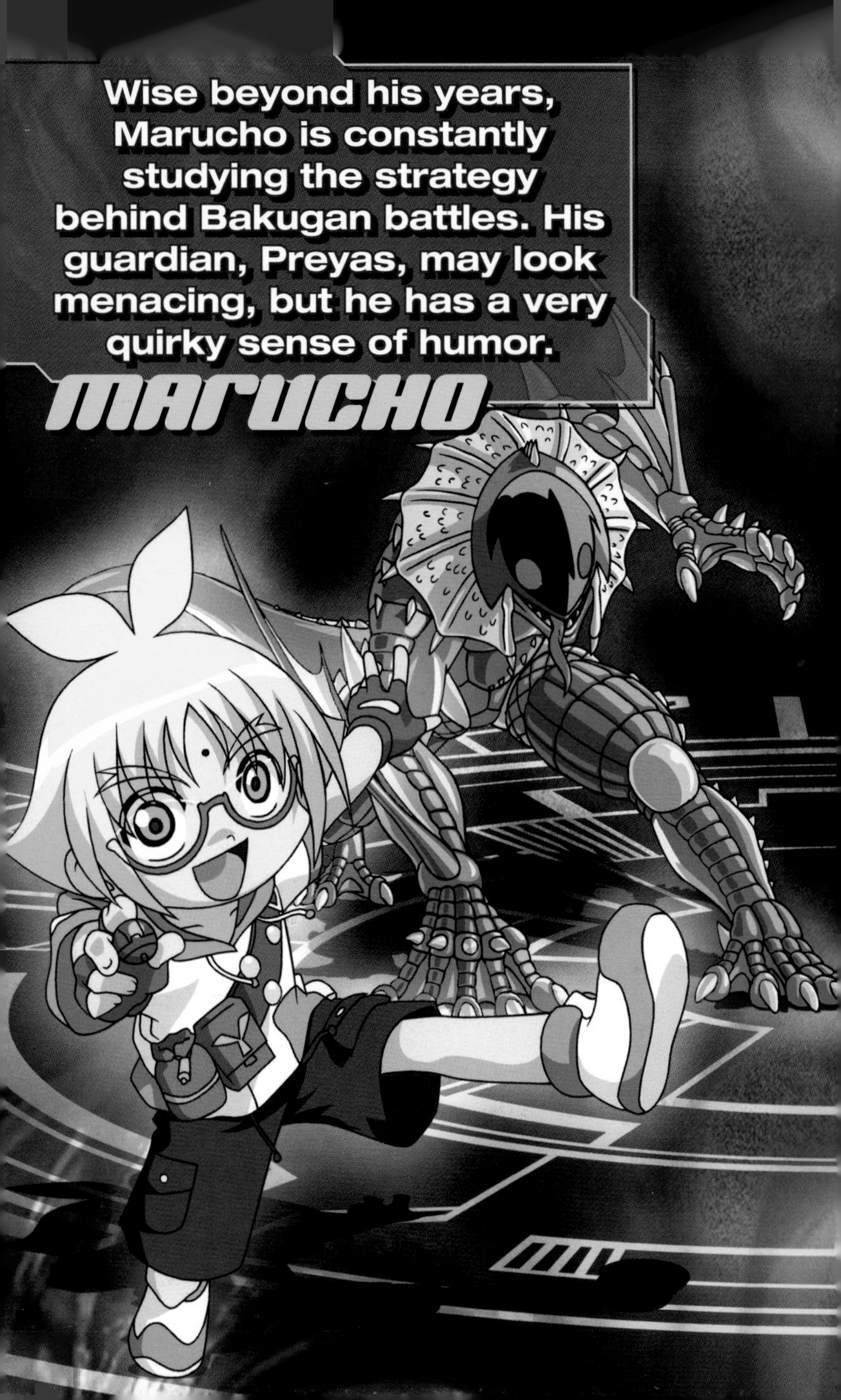

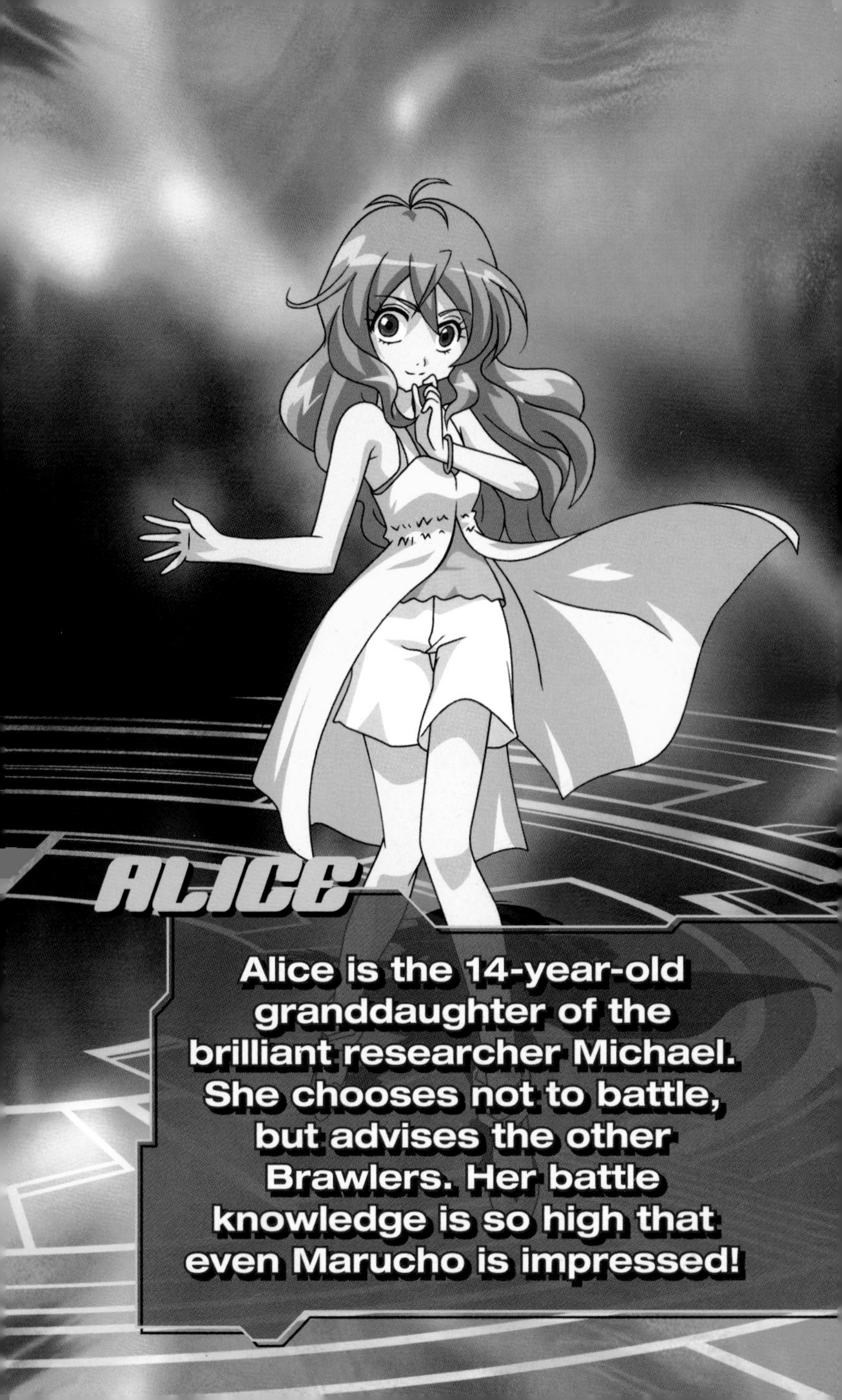

ALICE

Alice is the 14-year-old granddaughter of the brilliant researcher Michael. She chooses not to battle, but advises the other Brawlers. Her battle knowledge is so high that even Marucho is impressed!

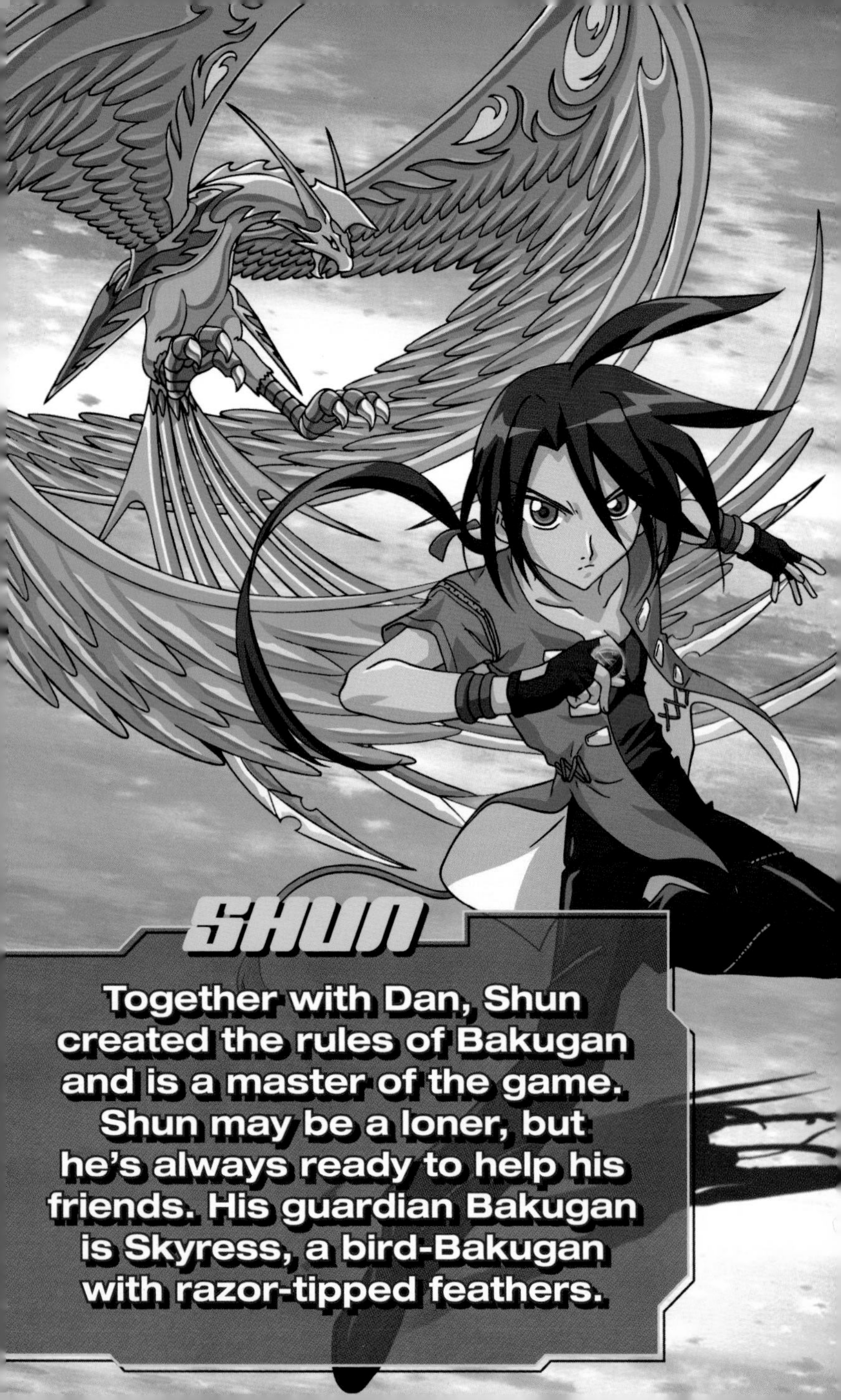

SHUN

Together with Dan, Shun created the rules of Bakugan and is a master of the game. Shun may be a loner, but he's always ready to help his friends. His guardian Bakugan is Skyress, a bird-Bakugan with razor-tipped feathers.

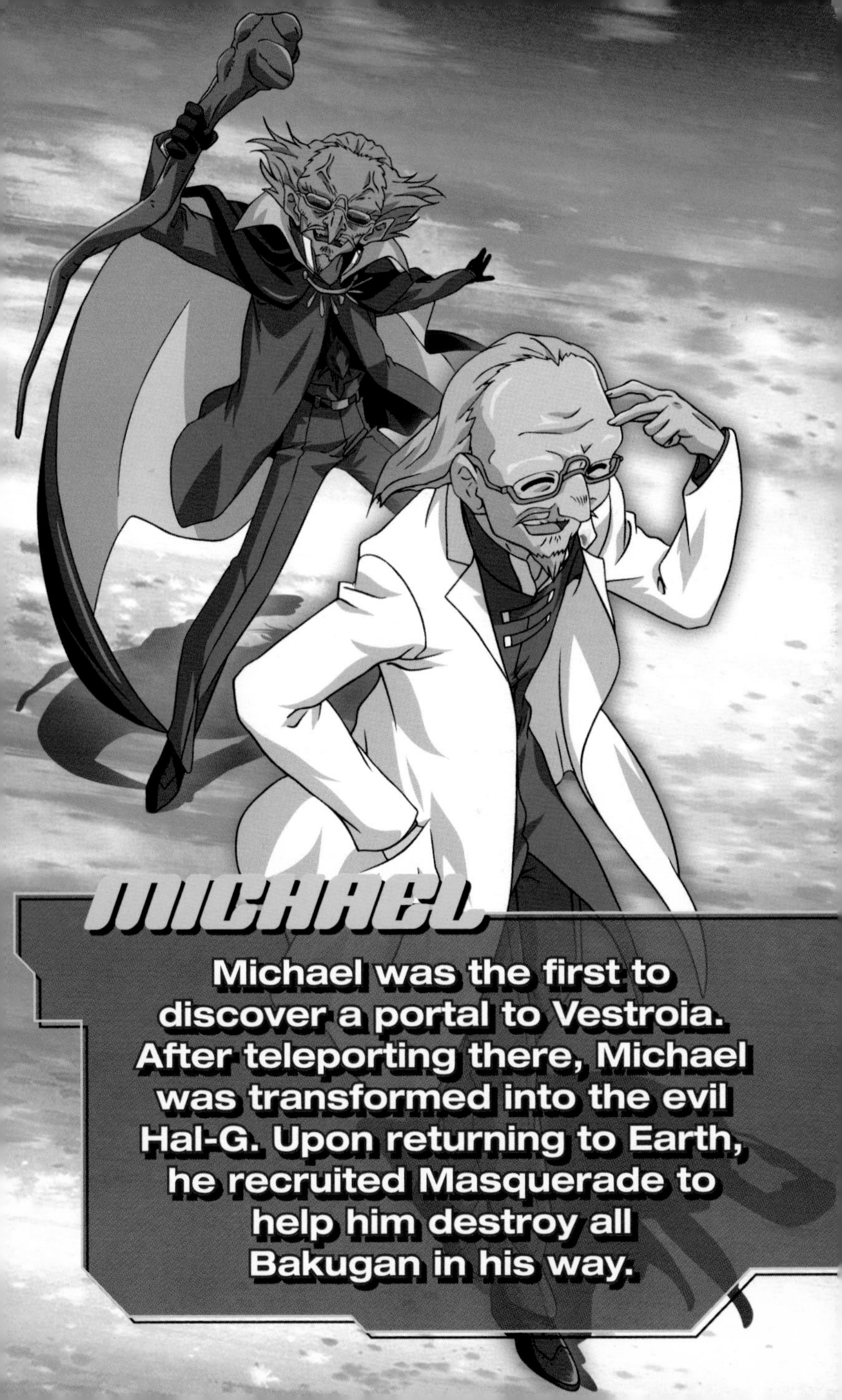

MICHAEL

Michael was the first to discover a portal to Vestroia. After teleporting there, Michael was transformed into the evil Hal-G. Upon returning to Earth, he recruited Masquerade to help him destroy all Bakugan in his way.

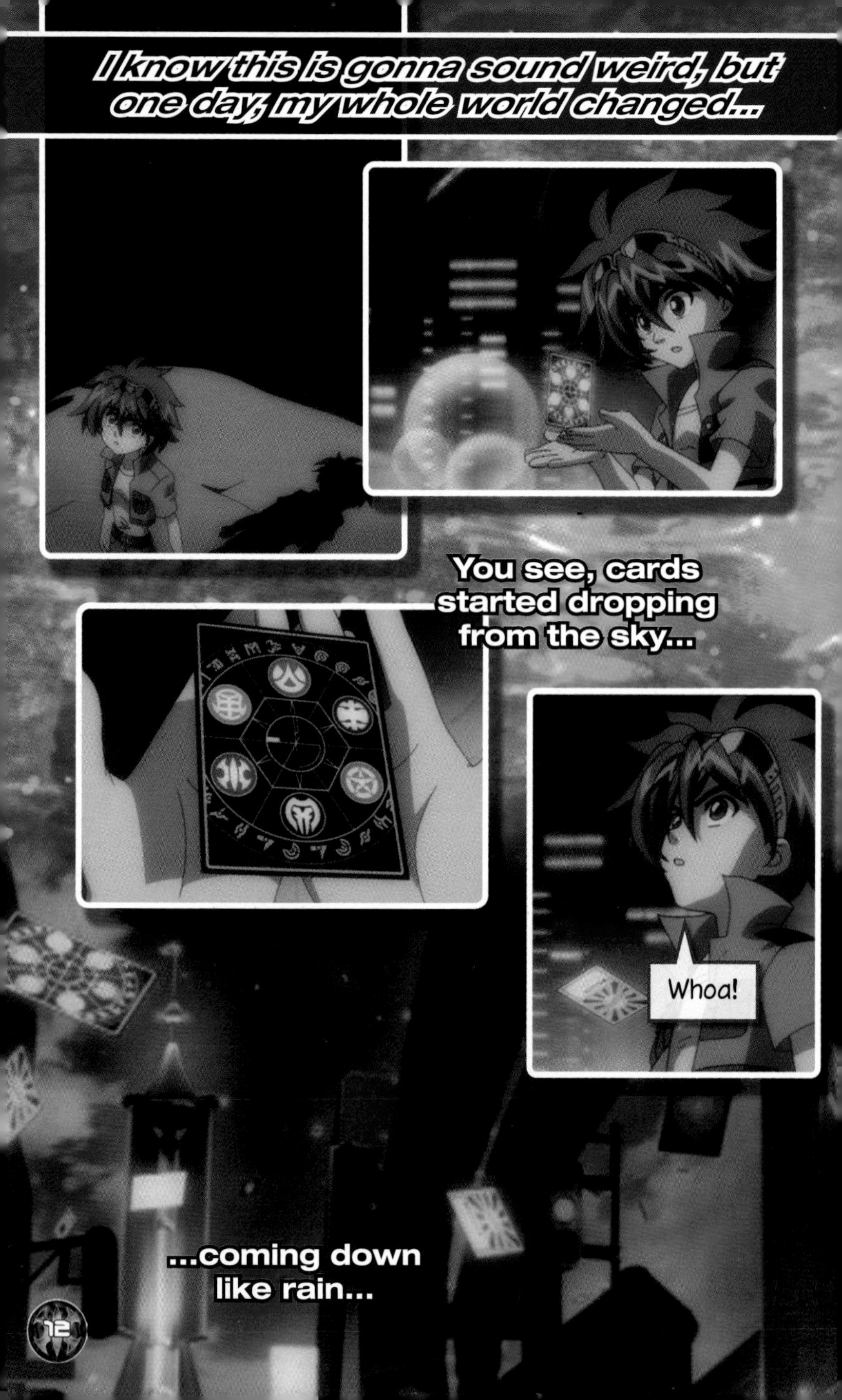
I know this is gonna sound weird, but one day, my whole world changed...
You see, cards started dropping from the sky...
Whoa!
...coming down like rain...
12

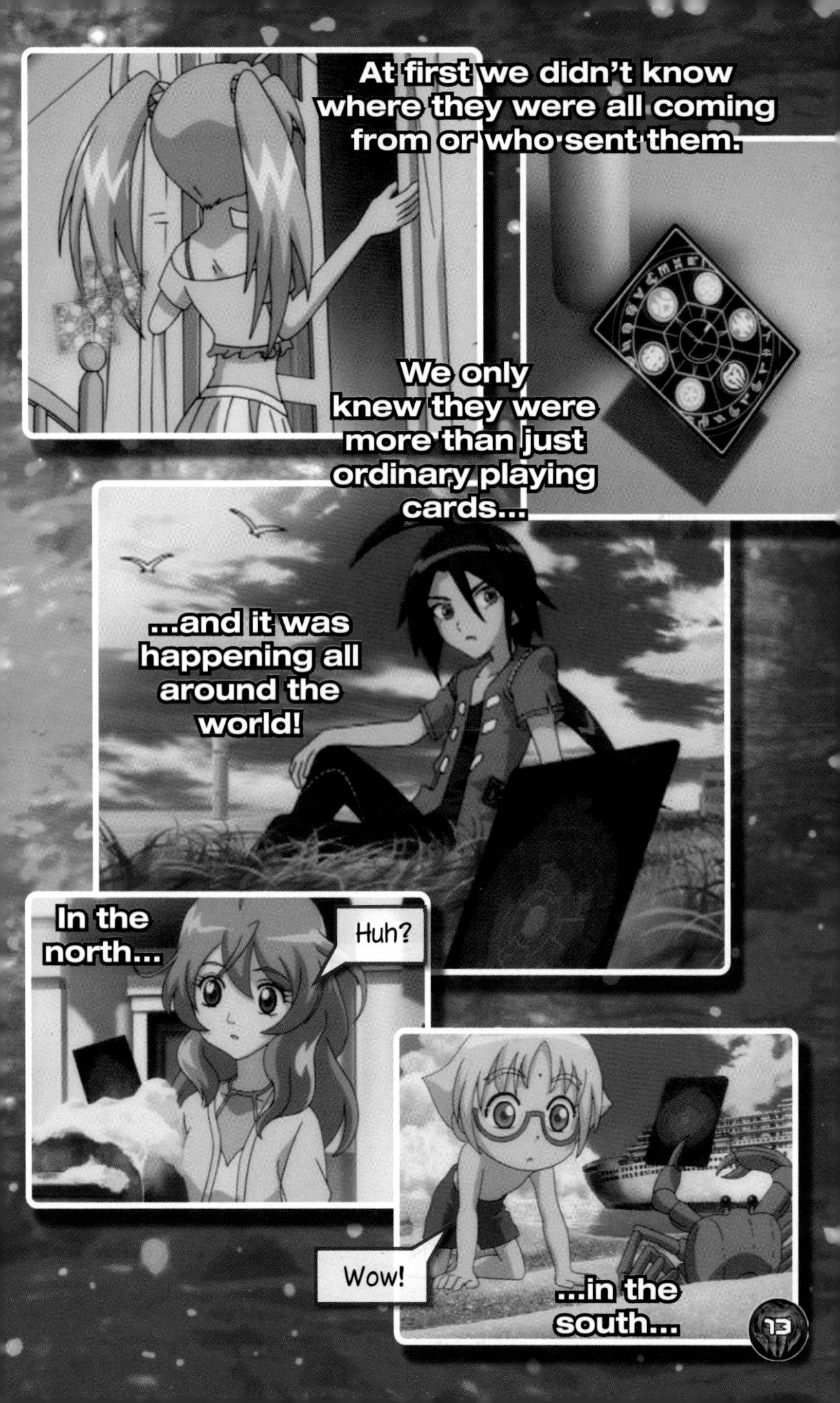
At first we didn't know where they were all coming from or who sent them.
We only knew they were more than just ordinary playing cards...
...and it was happening all around the world!
In the north...
Huh?
Wow!
...in the south...

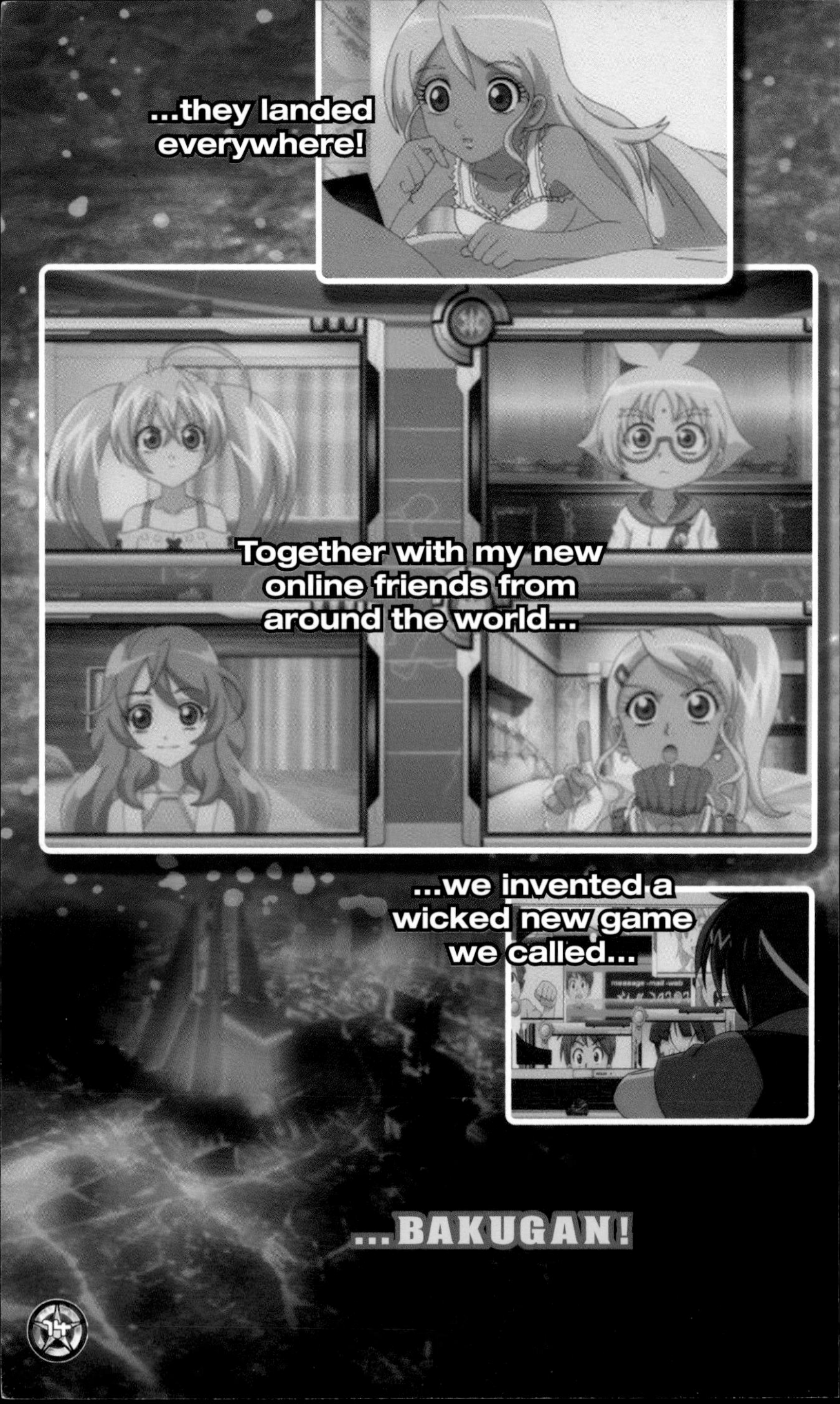
...they landed everywhere!
Together with my new online friends from around the world...
...we invented a wicked new game we called...
...BAKUGAN!

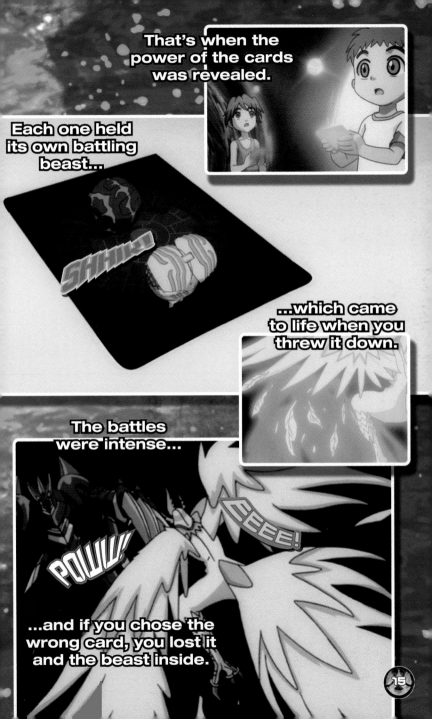

That's when the power of the cards was revealed.

Each one held its own battling beast...

SHHIP

...which came to life when you threw it down.

The battles were intense...

POW!!

EEEE!

...and if you chose the wrong card, you lost it and the beast inside.

15

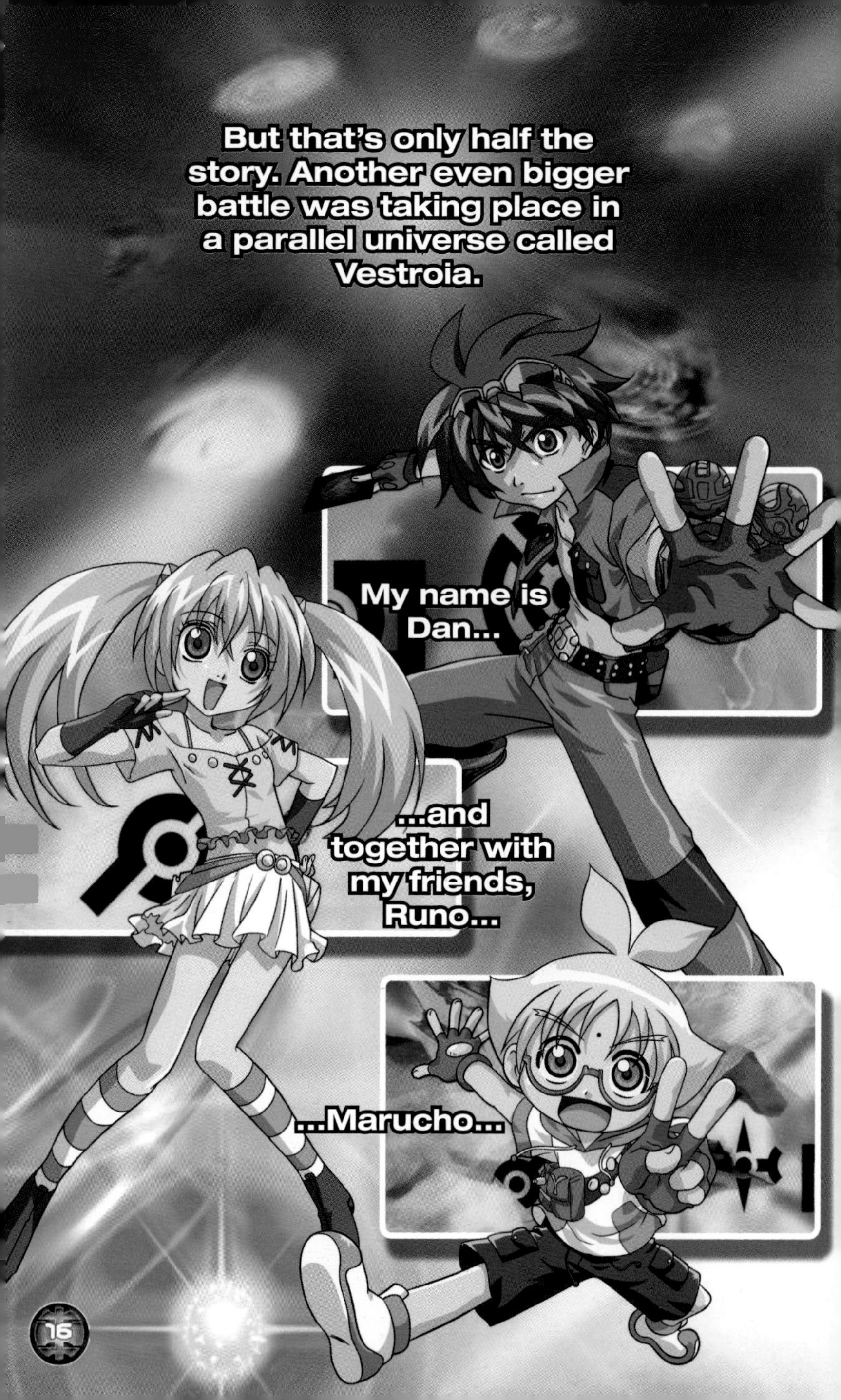
But that's only half the story. Another even bigger battle was taking place in a parallel universe called Vestroia.
My name is Dan...
...and together with my friends, Runo...
...Marucho...

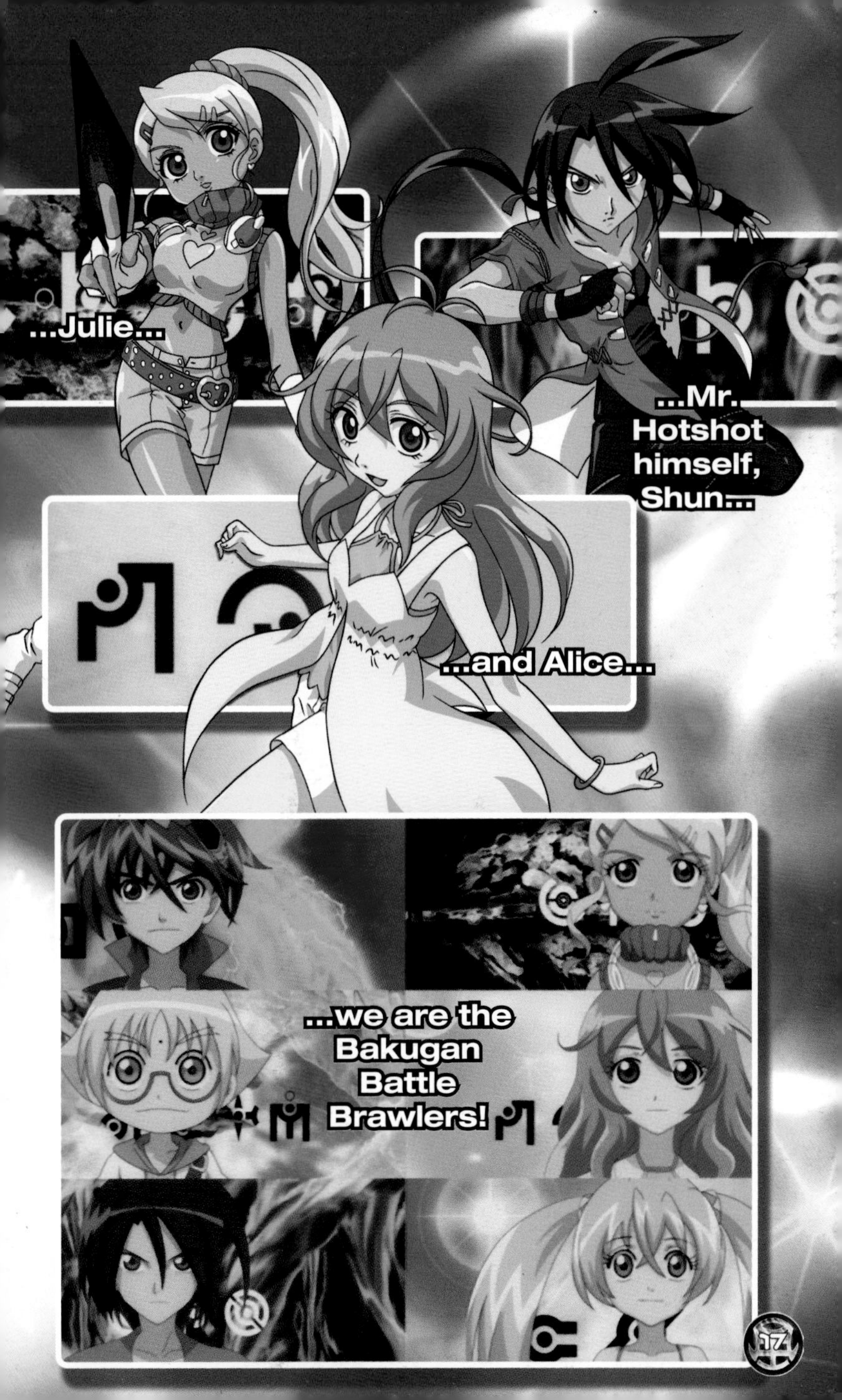

...Julie...
...Mr. Hotshot himself, Shun...
...and Alice...
...we are the Bakugan Battle Brawlers!

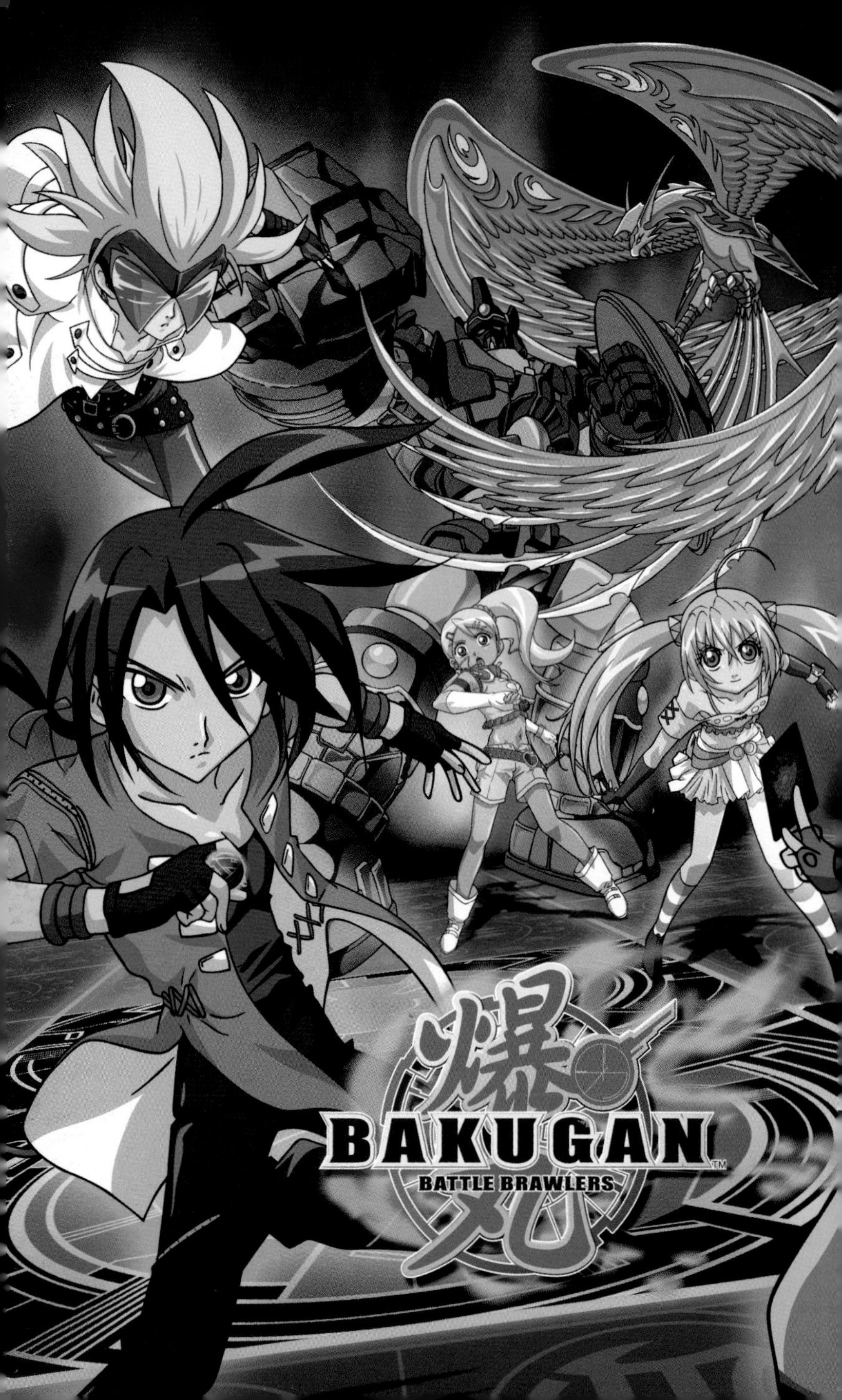

BAKUGAN
BATTLE BRAWLERS

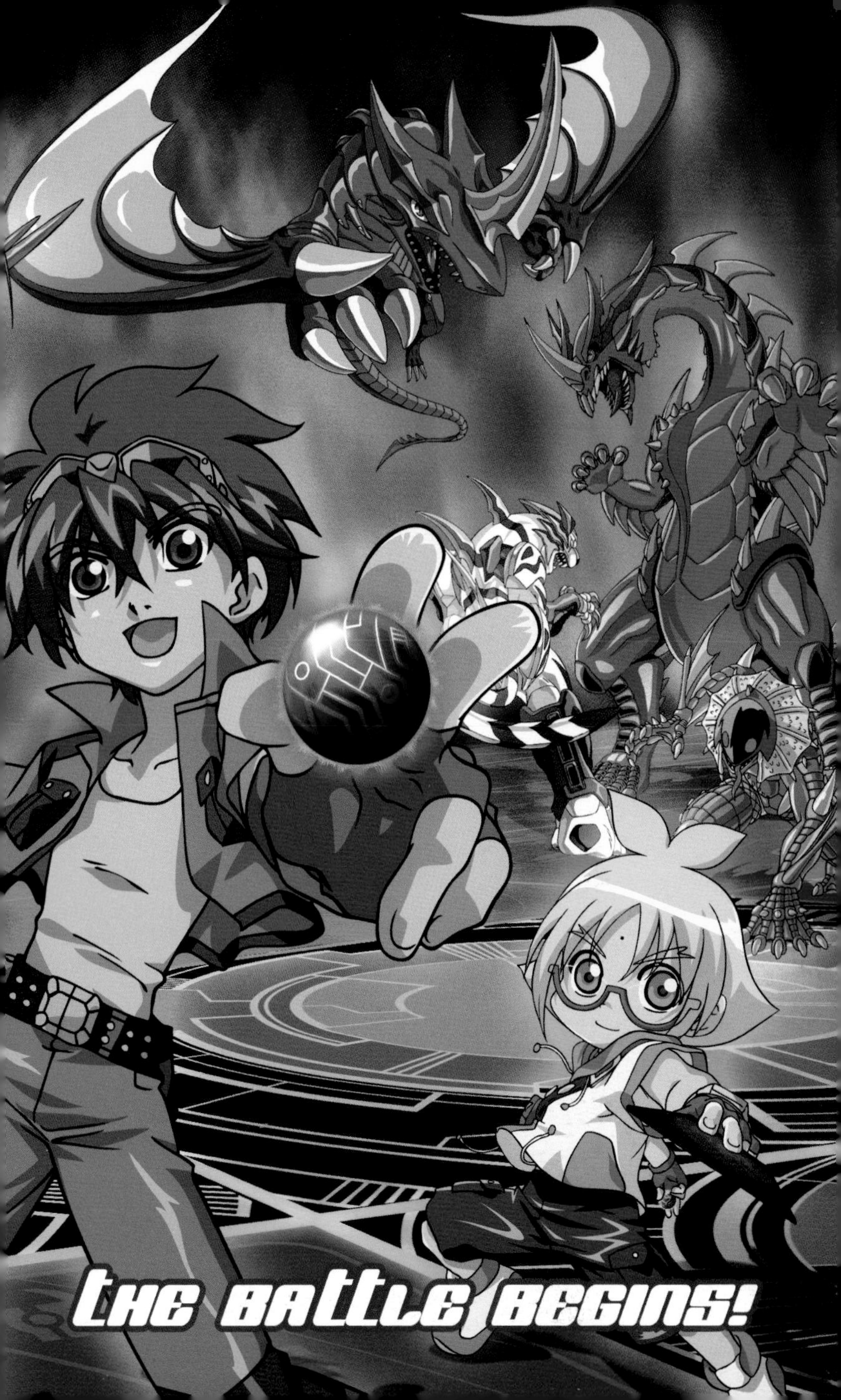
THE BATTLE BEGINS!

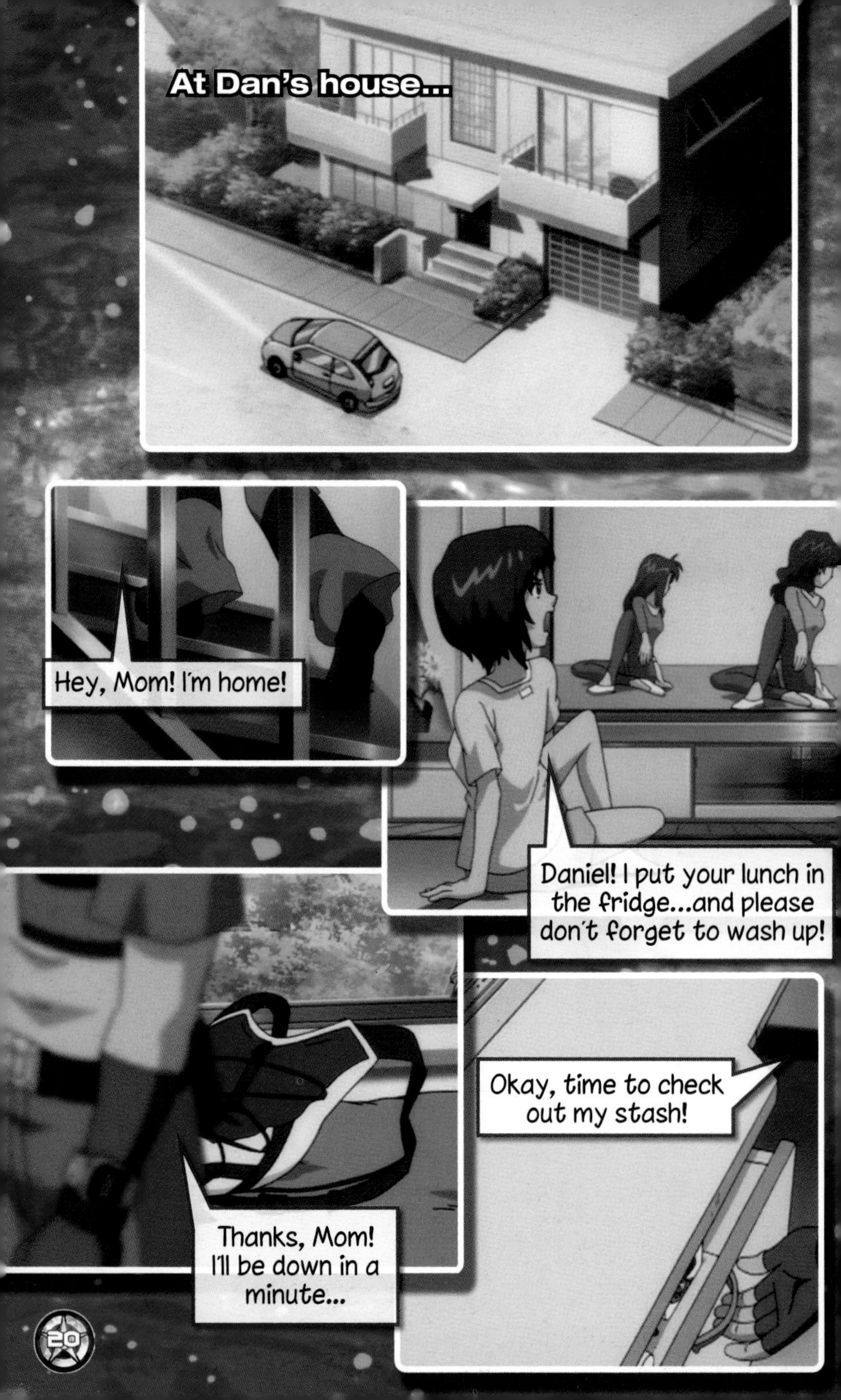

At Dan's house...
Hey, Mom! I'm home!
Daniel! I put your lunch in the fridge...and please don't forget to wash up!
Thanks, Mom! I'll be down in a minute...
Okay, time to check out my stash!

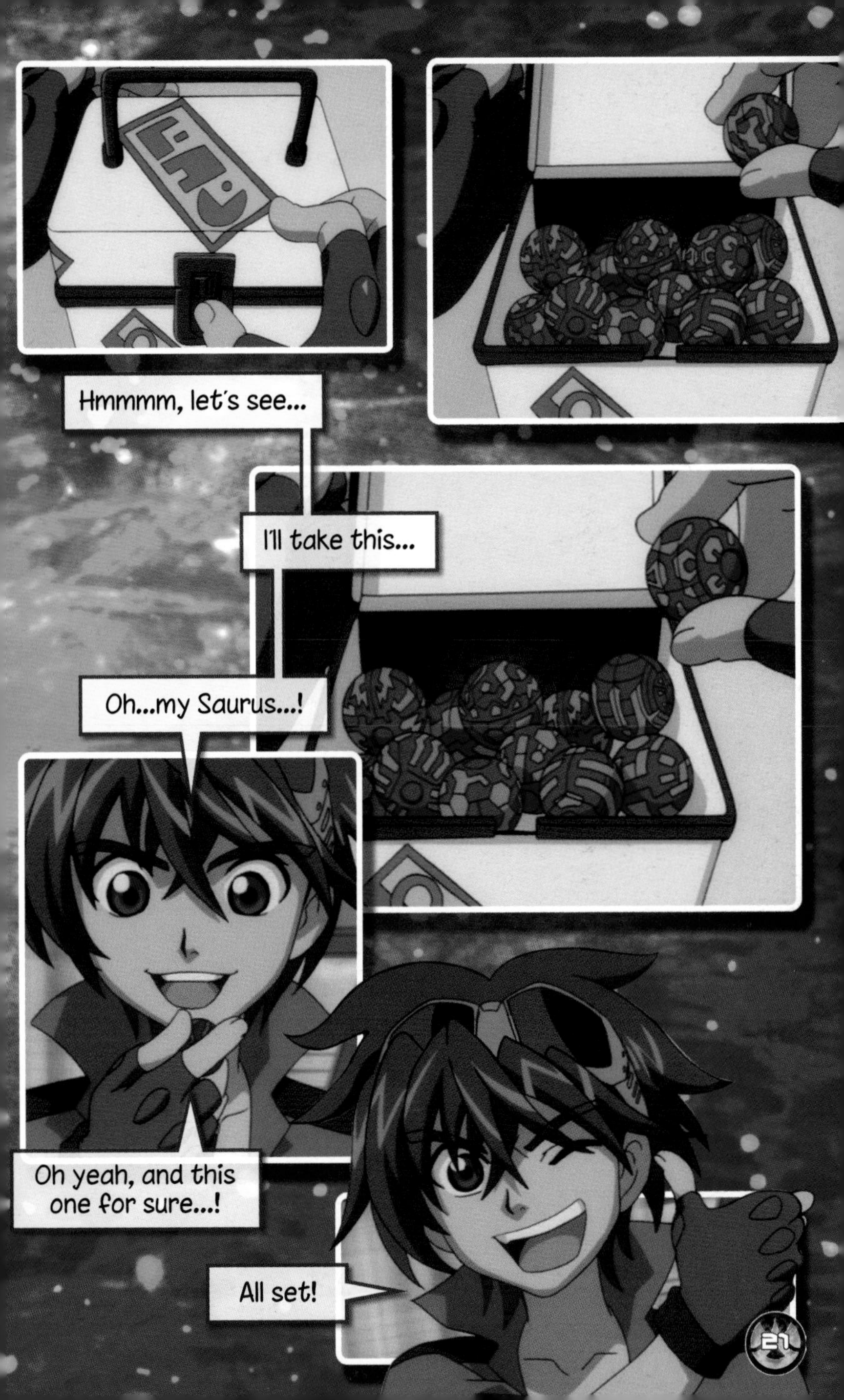
Hmmmm, let's see...
I'll take this...
Oh...my Saurus...!
Oh yeah, and this one for sure...!
All set!
21

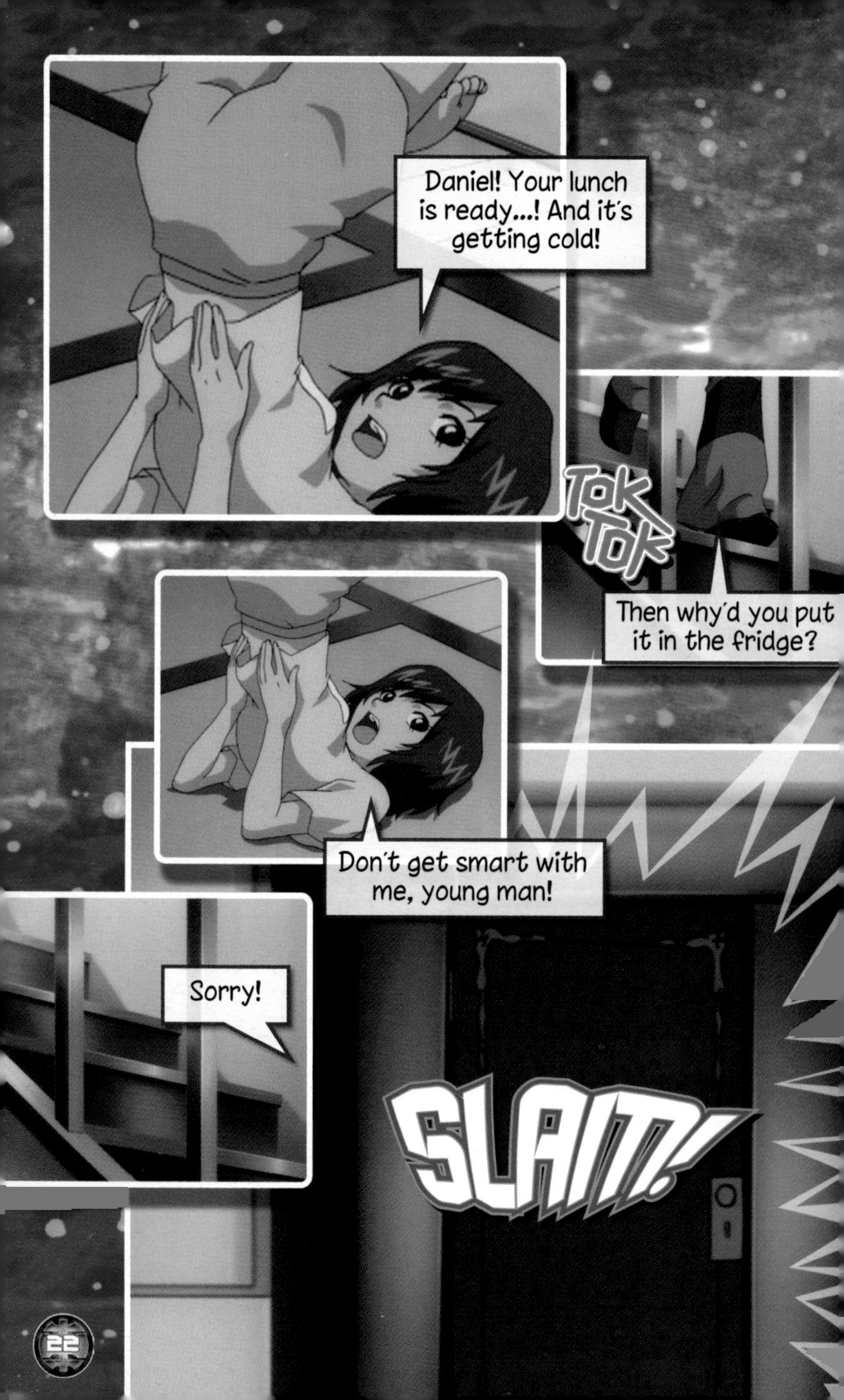
Daniel! Your lunch is ready...! And it's getting cold!
TOK TOK
Then why'd you put it in the fridge?
Don't get smart with me, young man!
Sorry!
SLAM!

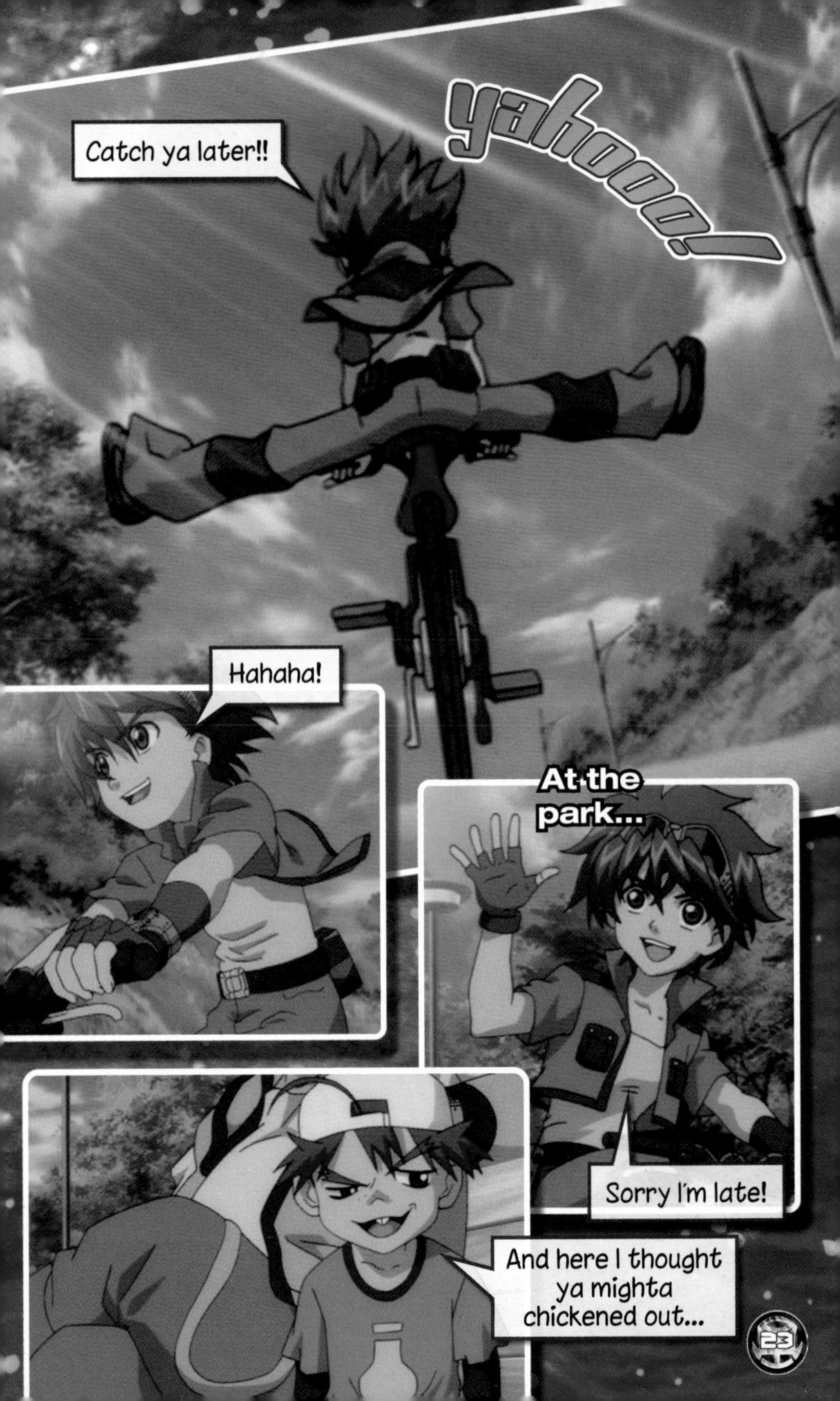

Catch ya later!!
yahooo!
Hahaha!
At the park...
Sorry I'm late!
And here I thought ya mighta chickened out...
23

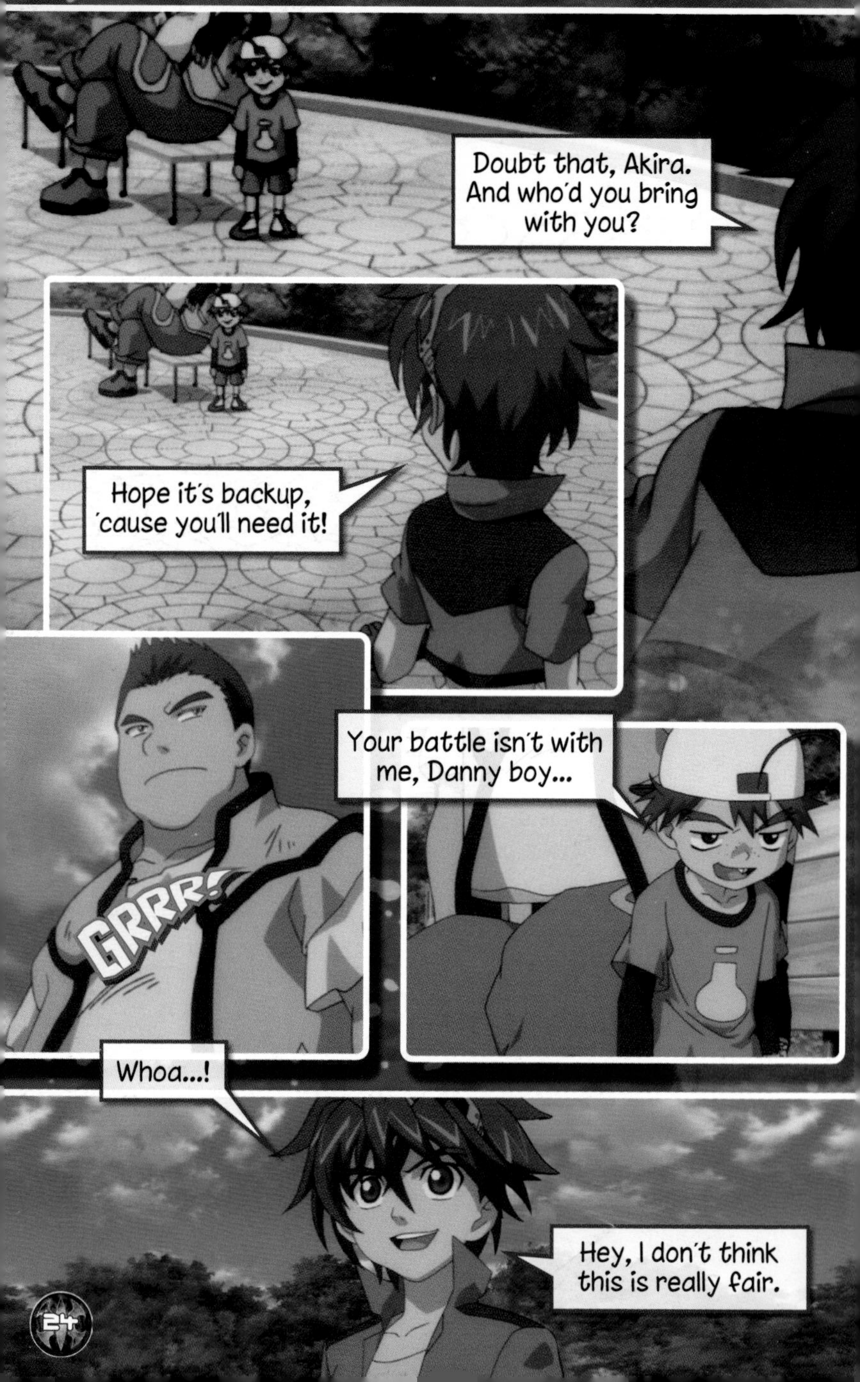
Doubt that, Akira. And who'd you bring with you?
Hope it's backup, 'cause you'll need it!
GRRR!
Your battle isn't with me, Danny boy...
Whoa...!
Hey, I don't think this is really fair.

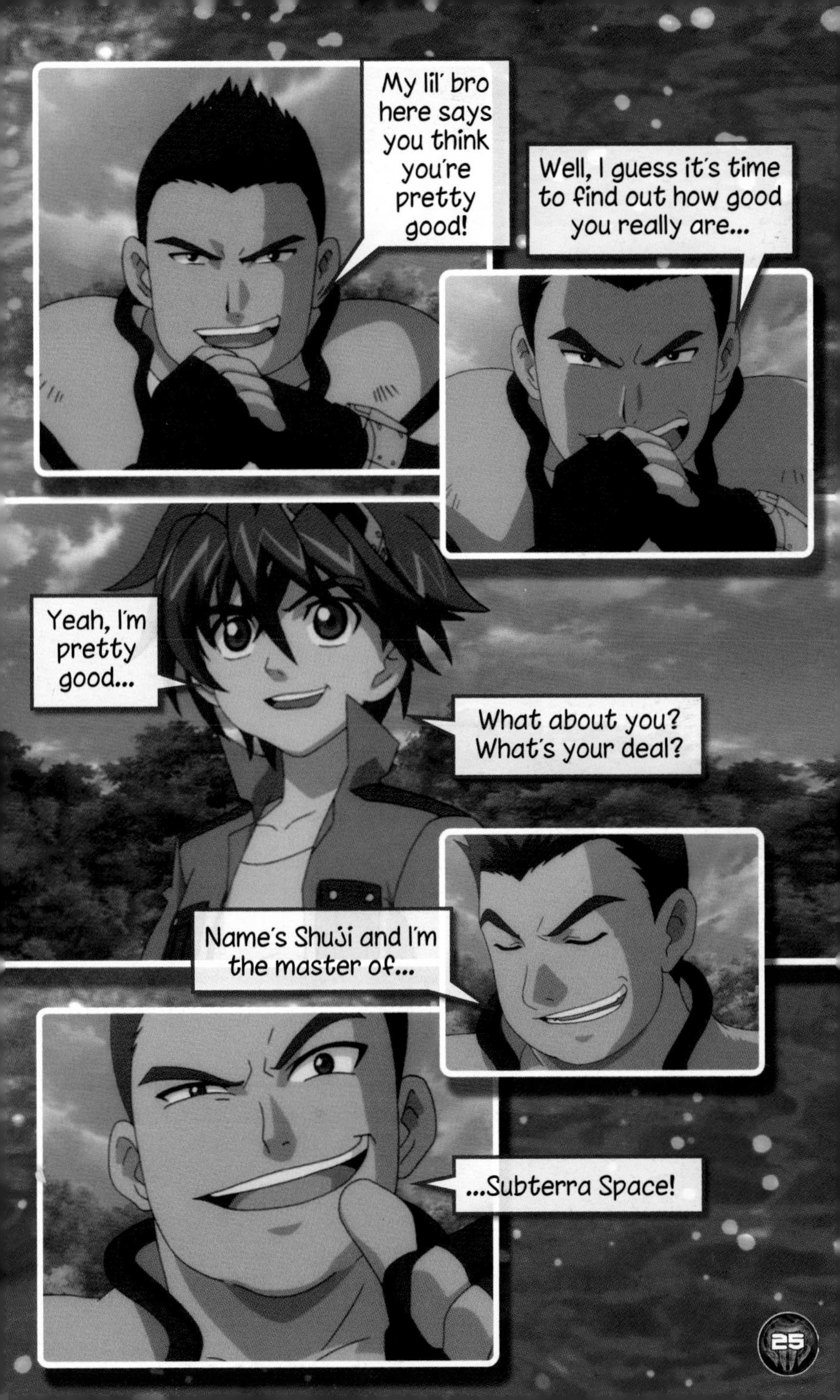
My lil' bro here says you think you're pretty good!
Well, I guess it's time to find out how good you really are...
Yeah, I'm pretty good...
What about you? What's your deal?
Name's Shuji and I'm the master of...
...Subterra Space!

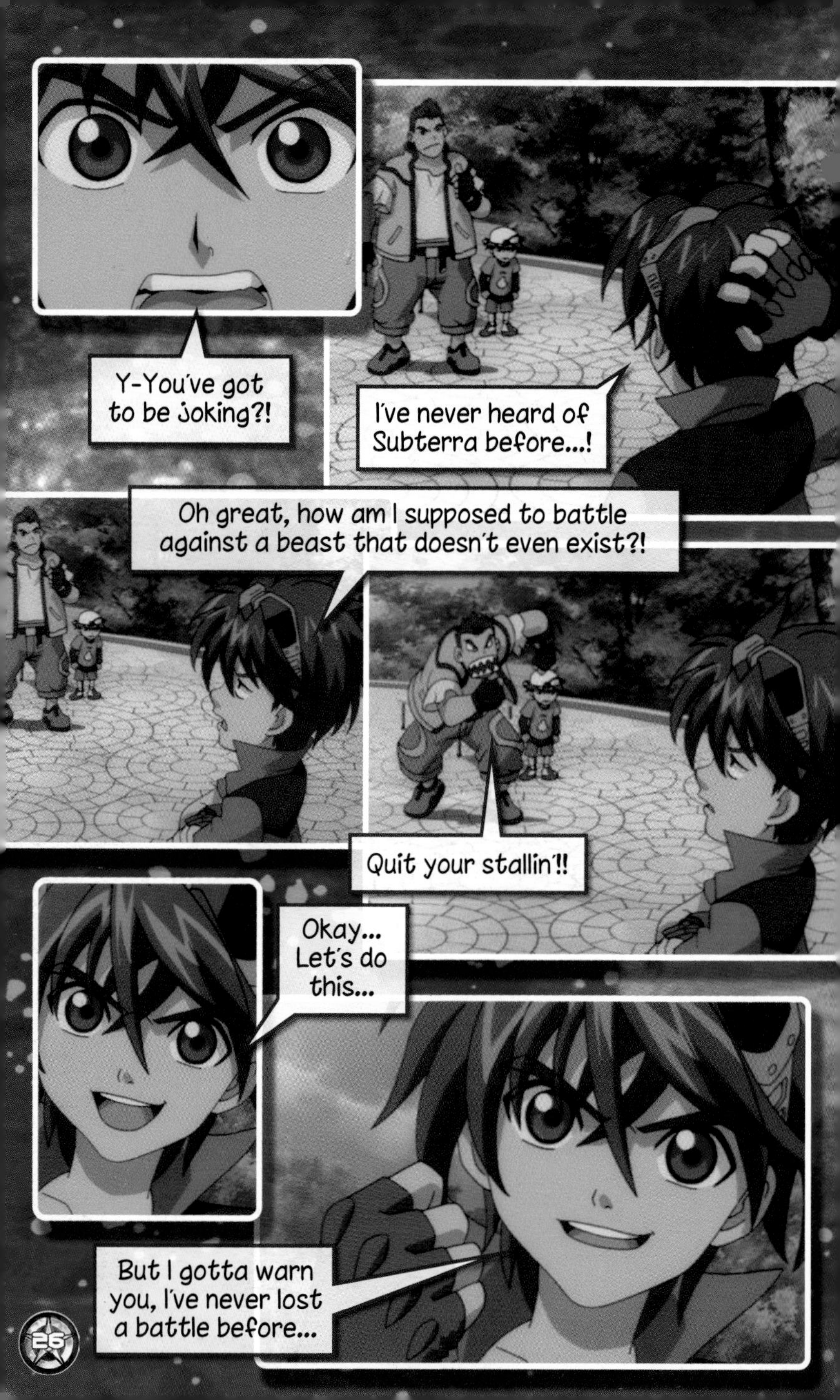
Y-You've got to be joking?!
I've never heard of Subterra before...!
Oh great, how am I supposed to battle against a beast that doesn't even exist?!
Quit your stallin'!!
Okay... Let's do this...
But I gotta warn you, I've never lost a battle before...

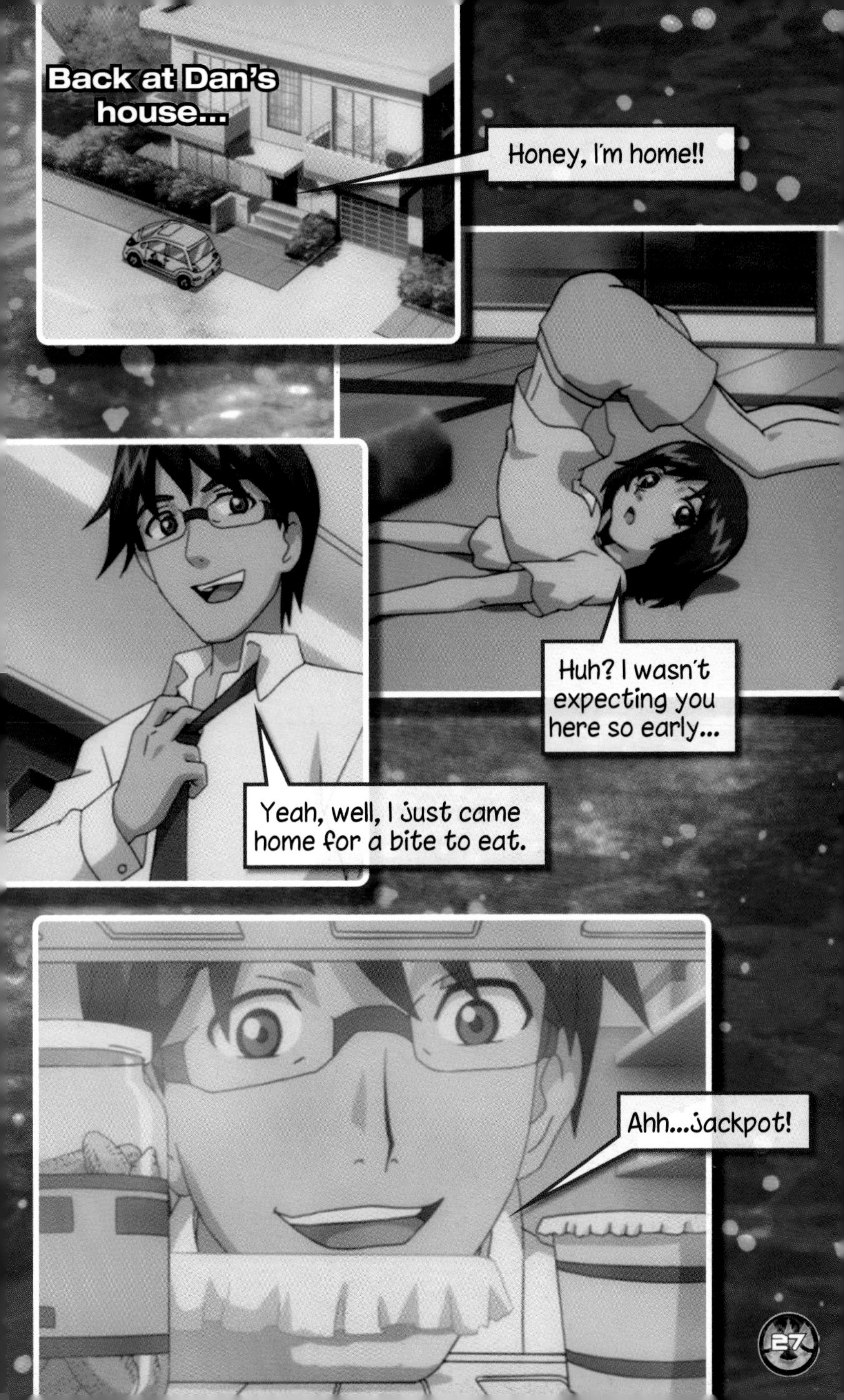
Back at Dan's house...
Honey, I'm home!!
Huh? I wasn't expecting you here so early...
Yeah, well, I just came home for a bite to eat.
Ahh...Jackpot!

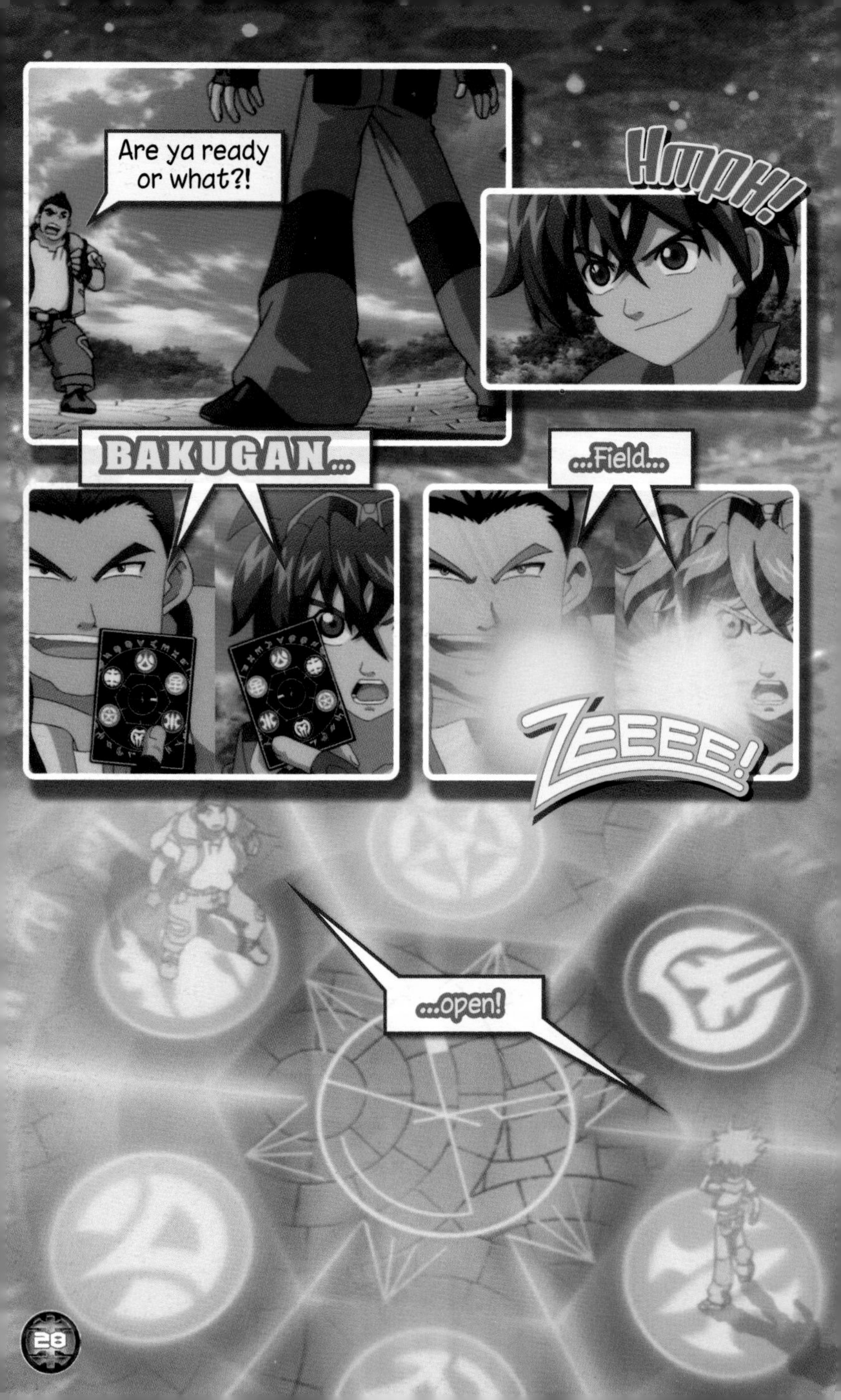

Are ya ready or what?!
HMPH!
BAKUGAN...
...Field...
ZEEEE!
...open!

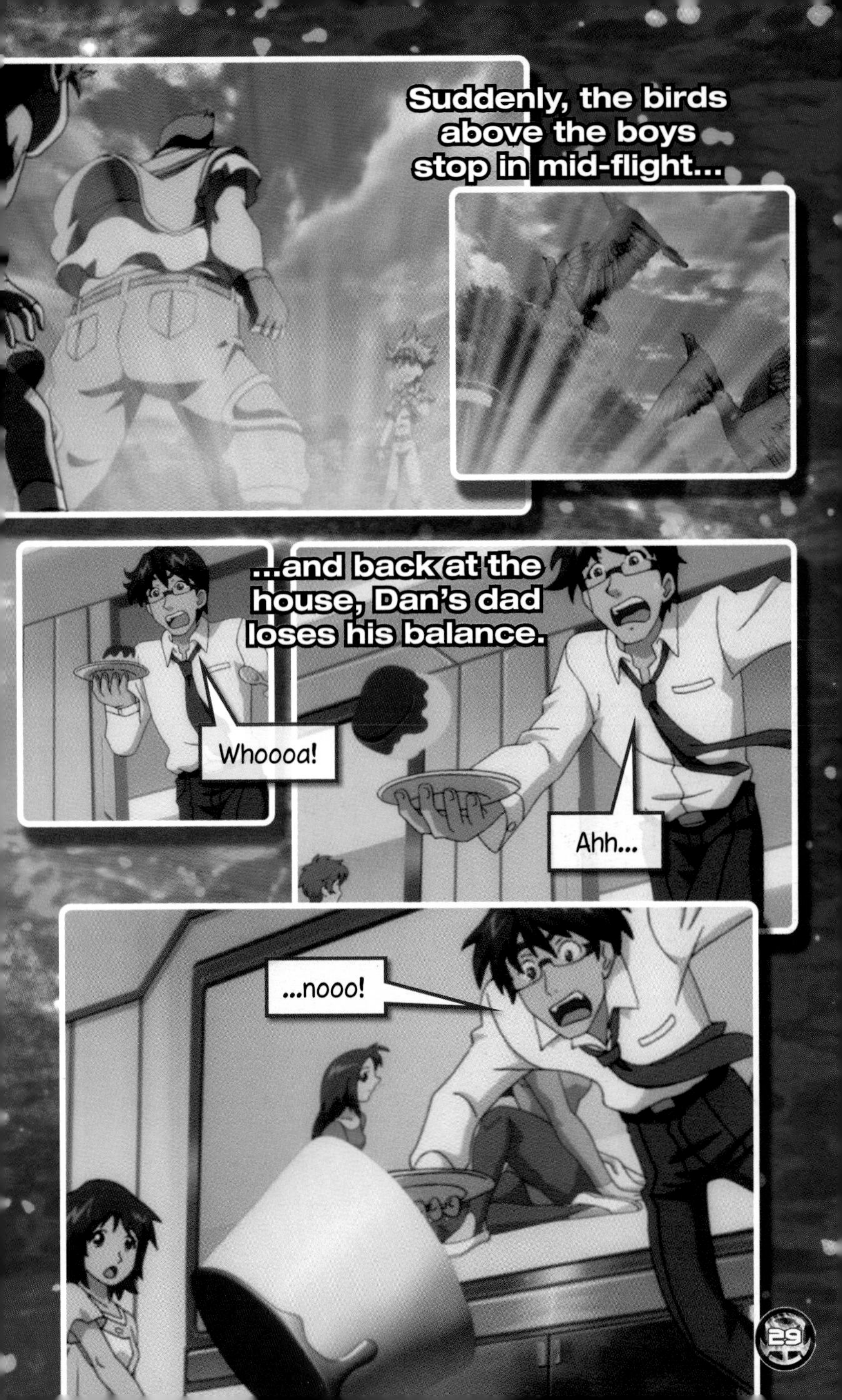

Suddenly, the birds above the boys stop in mid-flight...
...and back at the house, Dan's dad loses his balance.
Whoooa!
Ahh...
...nooo!

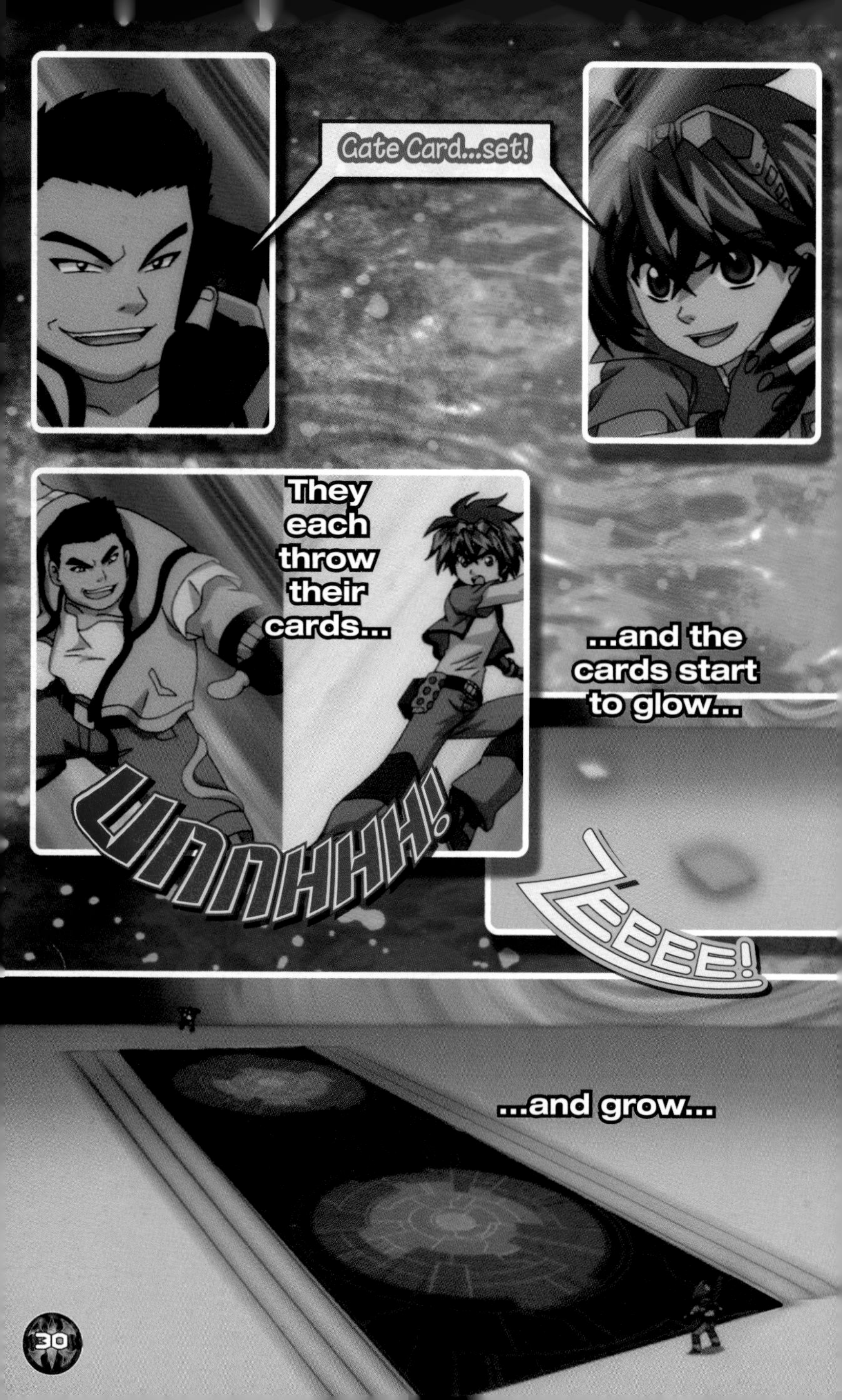
Gate Card...set!
They each throw their cards...
WAAHHH!
...and the cards start to glow...
ZEEEE!
...and grow...

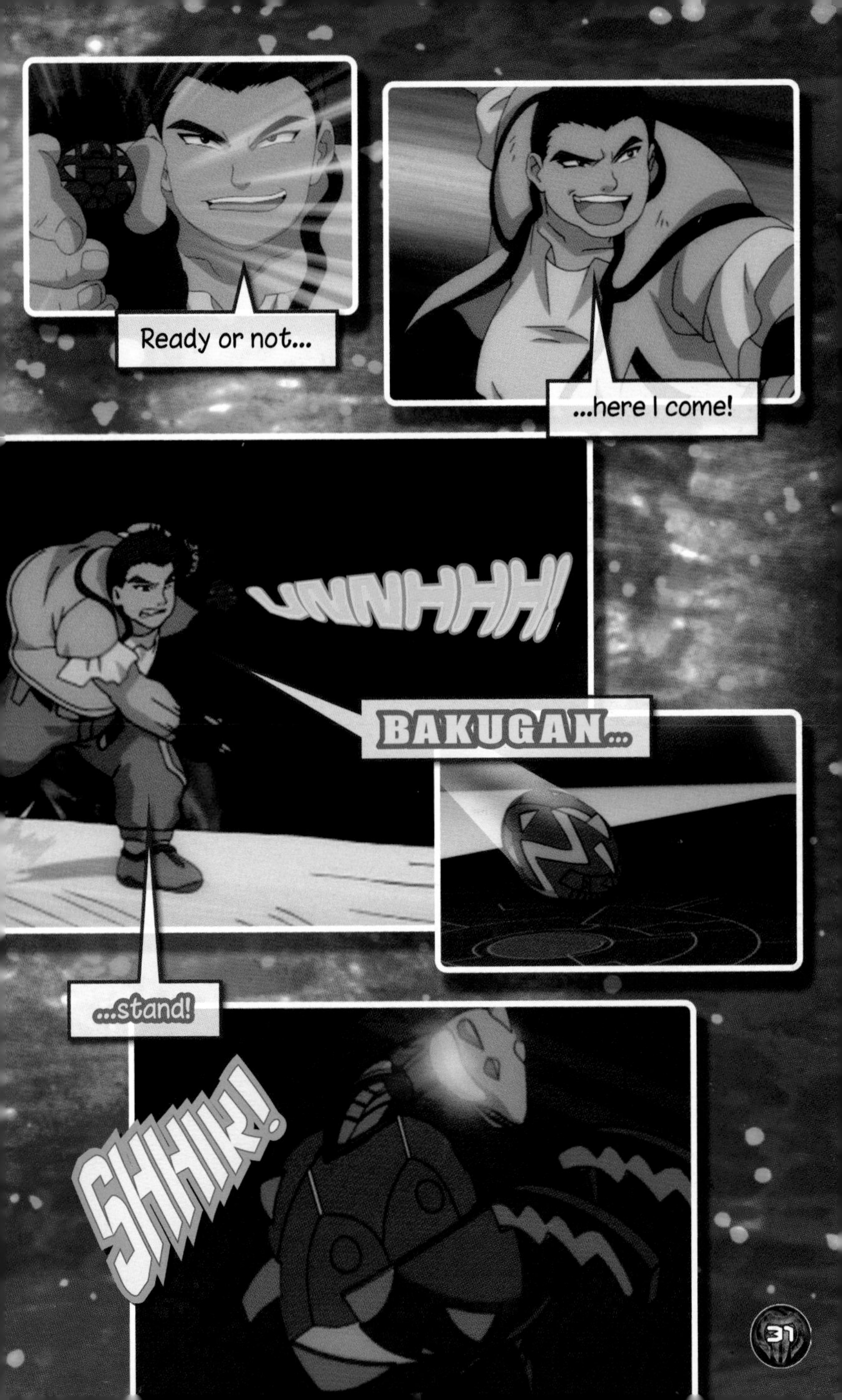

Ready or not...
...here I come!
UNNHHH!
BAKUGAN...
...stand!
SHHK!

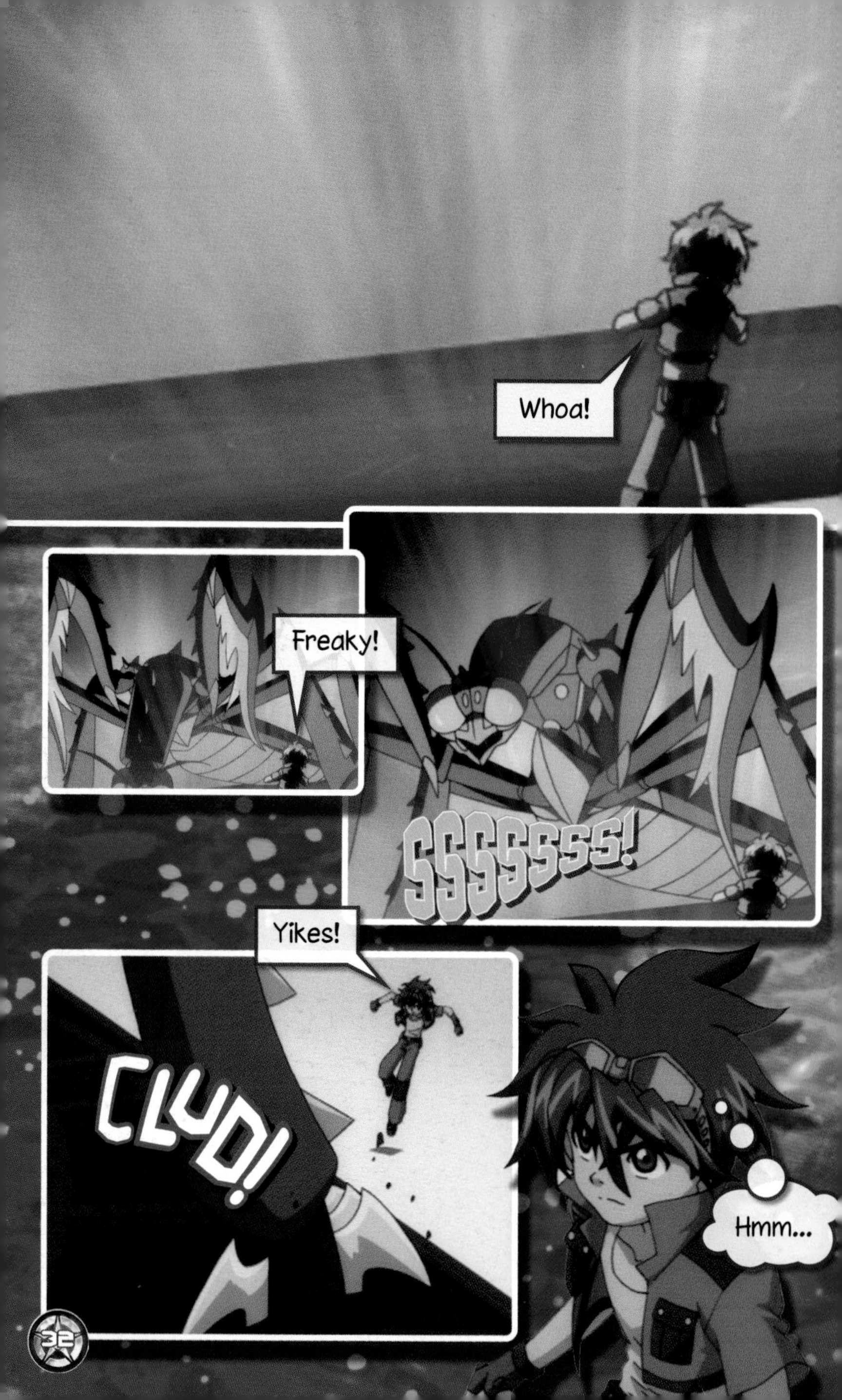

Whoa!
Freaky!
SSSSSSS!
Yikes!
CLUD!
Hmm...

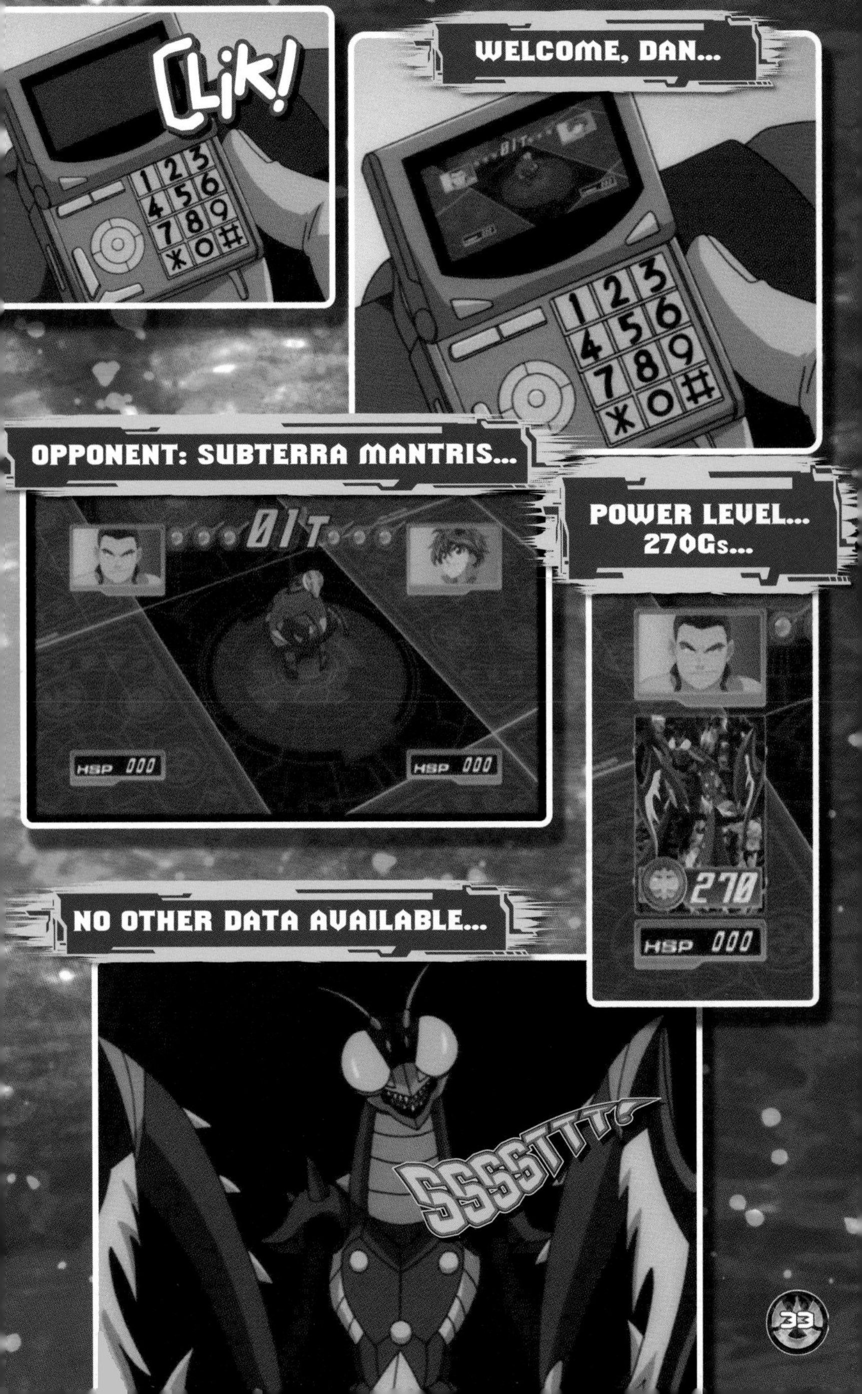
CLIK!
WELCOME, DAN...
OPPONENT: SUBTERRA MANTRIS...
01T
HSP 000
HSP 000
POWER LEVEL...
270Gs...
270
HSP 000
NO OTHER DATA AVAILABLE...
SSSSTTTT

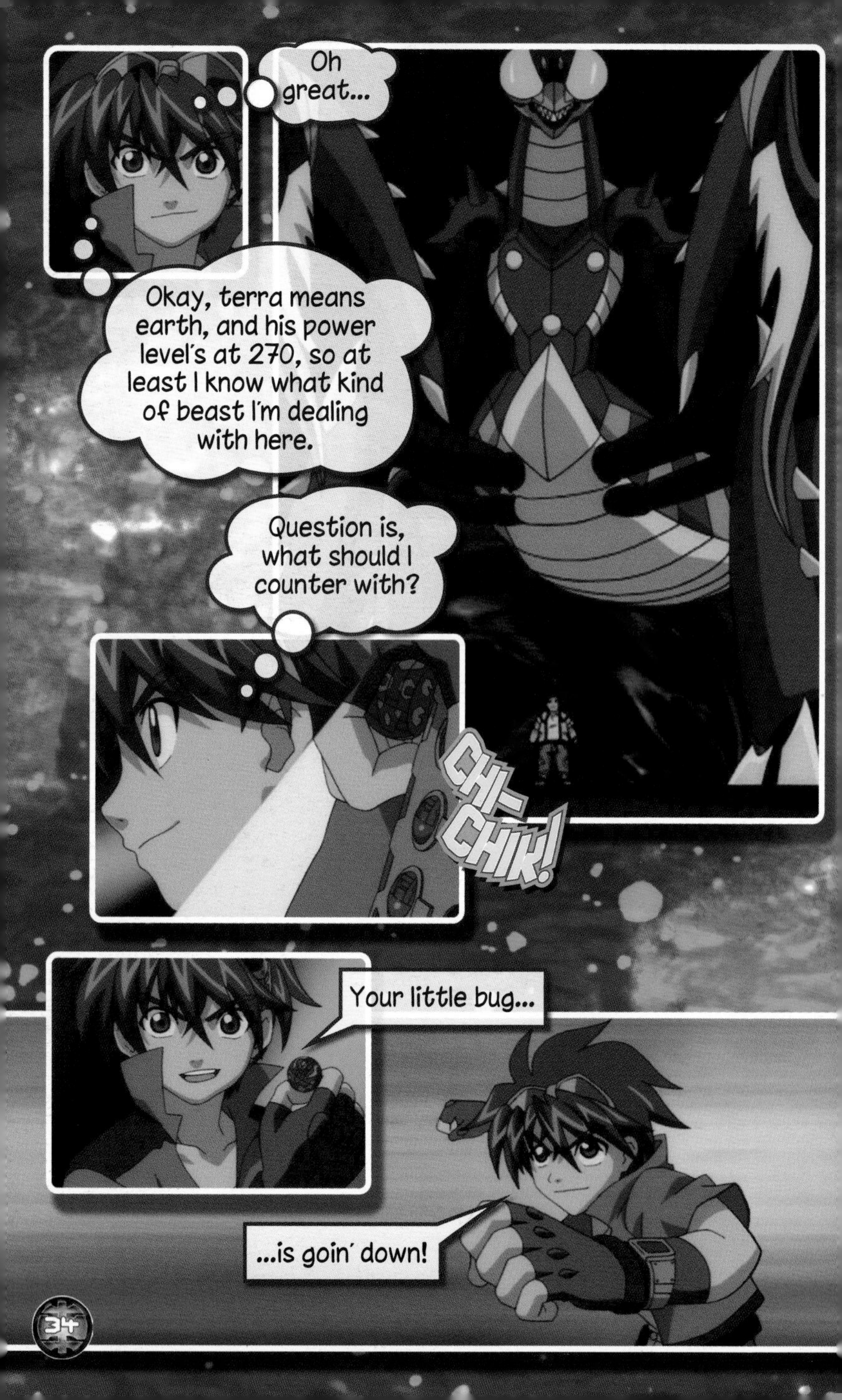
Oh great...
Okay, terra means earth, and his power level's at 270, so at least I know what kind of beast I'm dealing with here.
Question is, what should I counter with?
CHI-CHIK!
Your little bug...
...is goin' down!

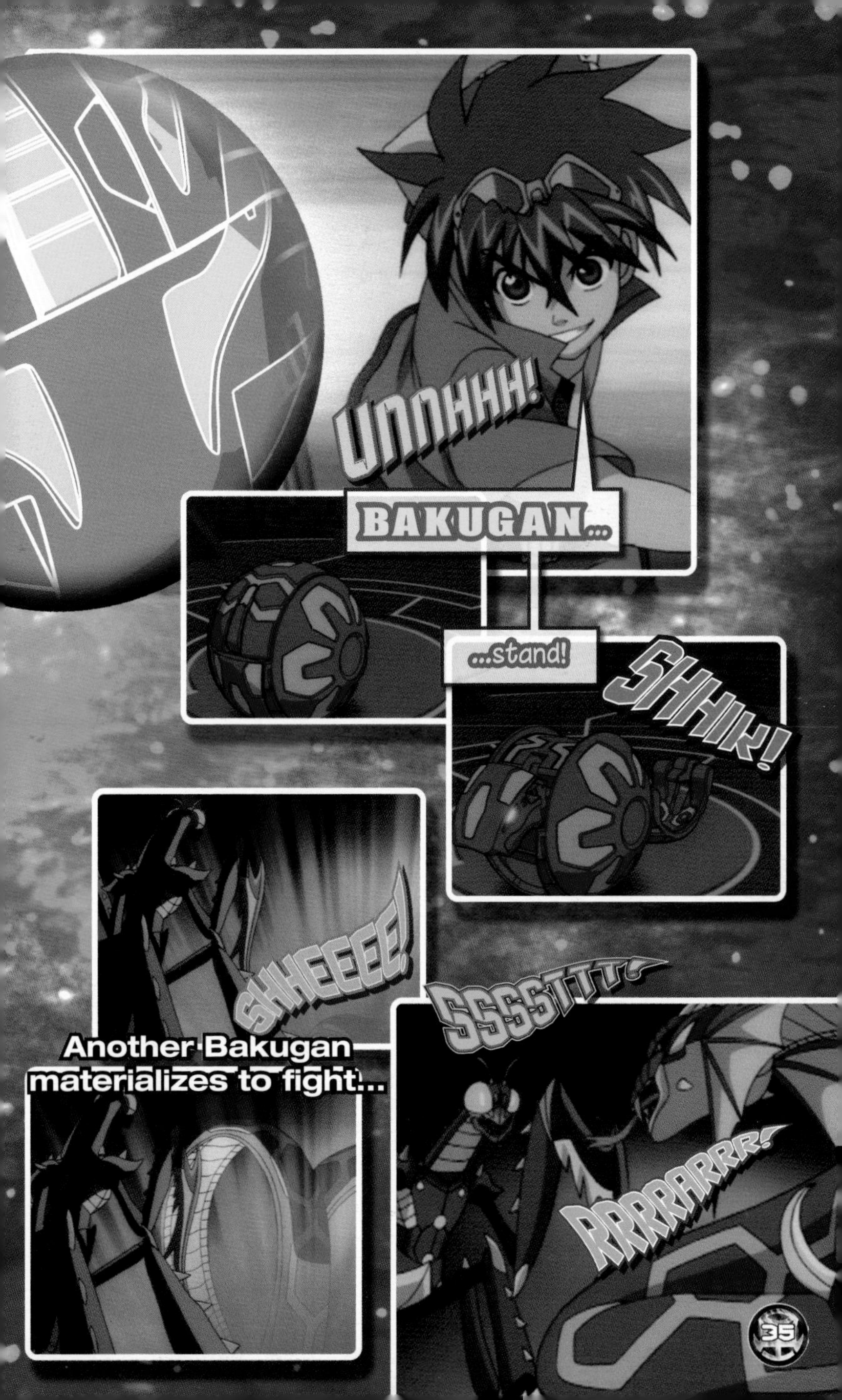
UNNHHH!
BAKUGAN...
...stand!
SHHIK!
SHHEEEE!
Another Bakugan materializes to fight...
SSSSTTTT!
RRRRARRR!

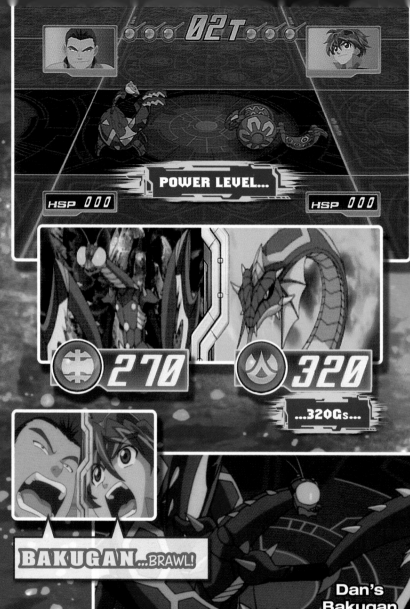

02T

POWER LEVEL...

HSP 000

HSP 000

270

320

...320Gs...

BAKUGAN...BRAWL!

Dan's Bakugan quickly winds around Shuji's...

36

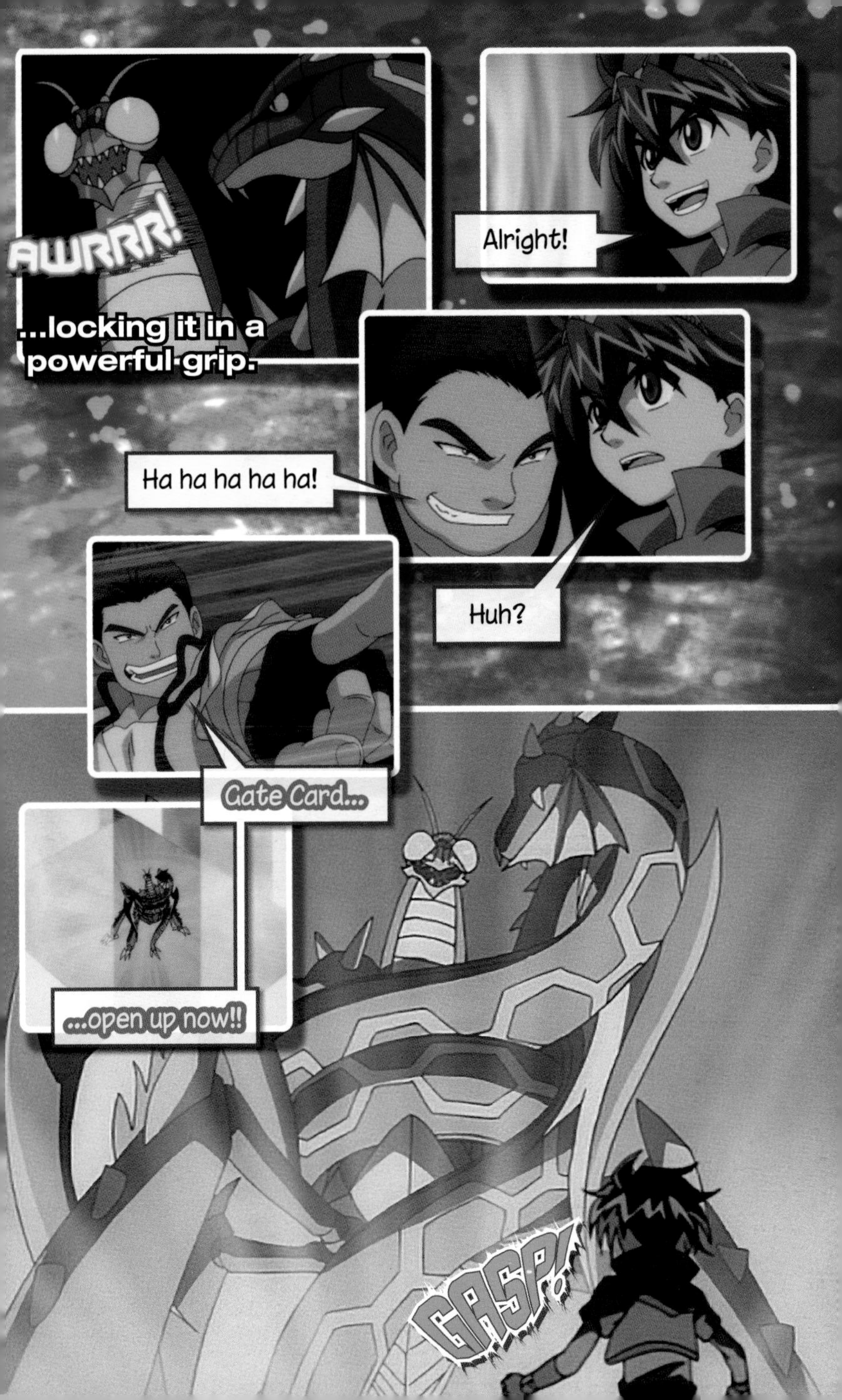
AWRRR!
...locking it in a powerful grip.
Alright!
Ha ha ha ha ha!
Huh?
Gate Card...
...open up now!!
GASP!

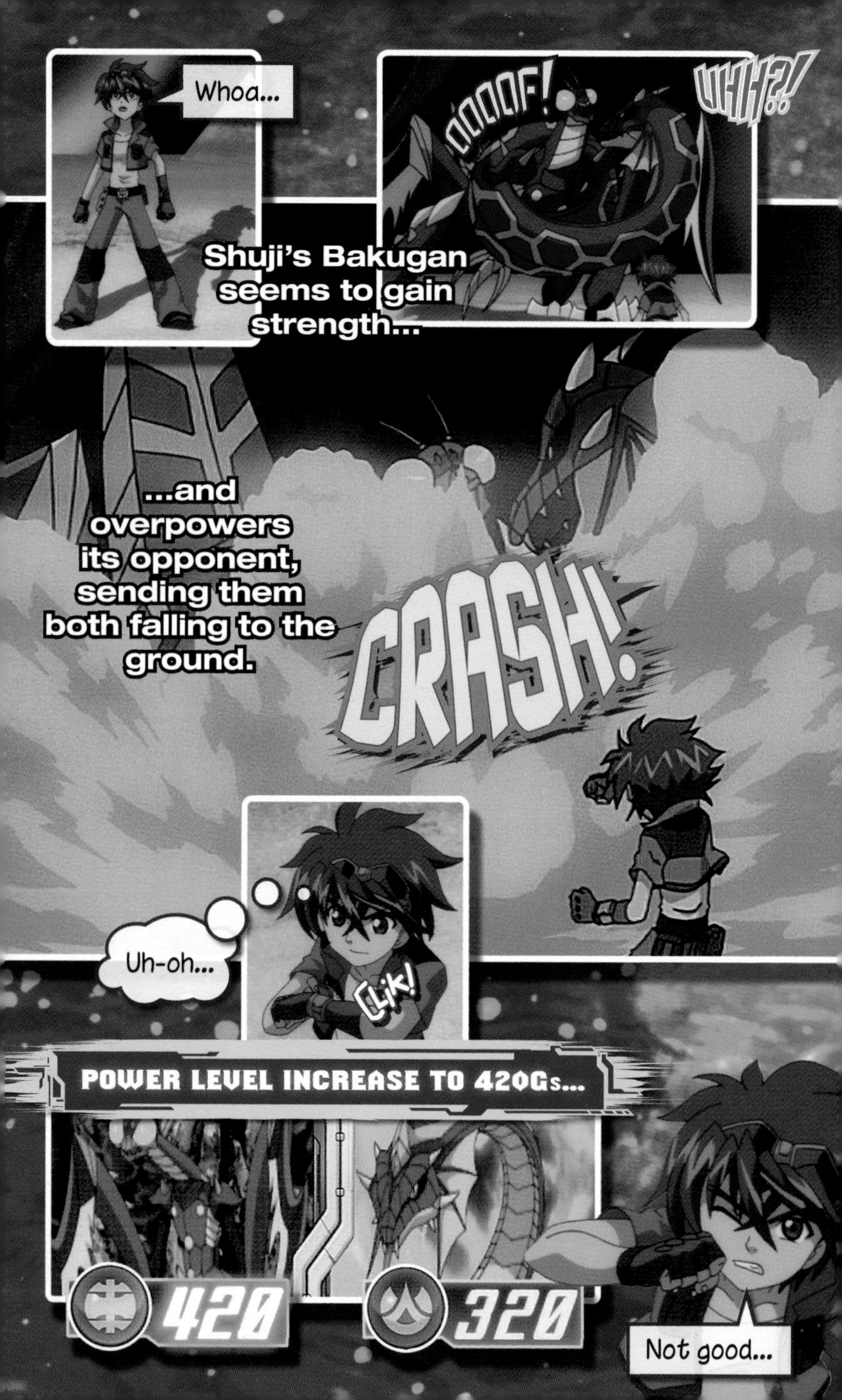
Whoa...
OOOOF!
UHH?!
Shuji's Bakugan seems to gain strength...
...and overpowers its opponent, sending them both falling to the ground.
CRASH!
Uh-oh...
CLIK!
POWER LEVEL INCREASE TO 420Gs...
420
320
Not good...

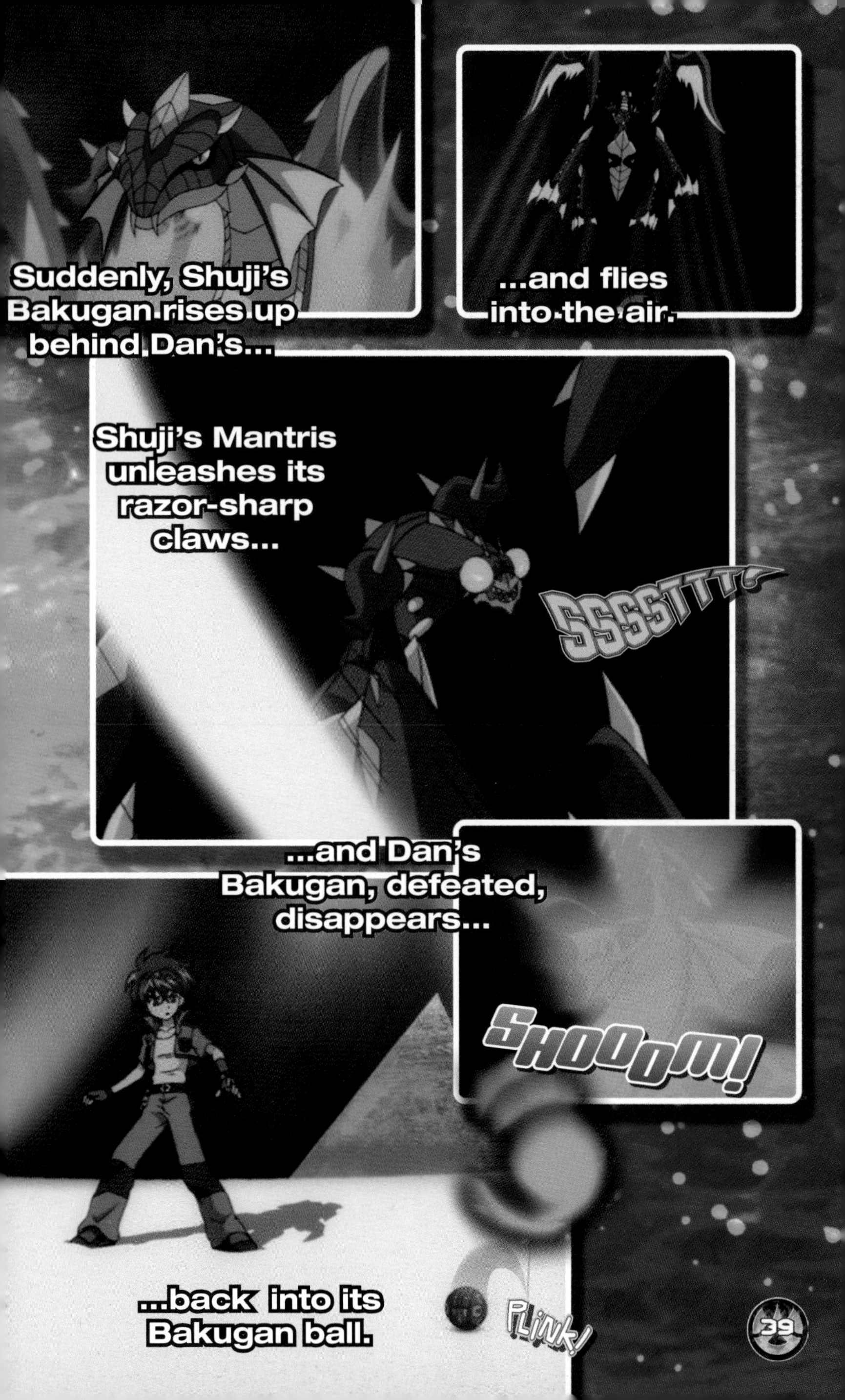
Suddenly, Shuji's Bakugan rises up behind Dan's...
...and flies into the air.
Shuji's Mantris unleashes its razor-sharp claws...
SSSSTTTT
...and Dan's Bakugan, defeated, disappears...
SHOOOM!
...back into its Bakugan ball.
PLINK!

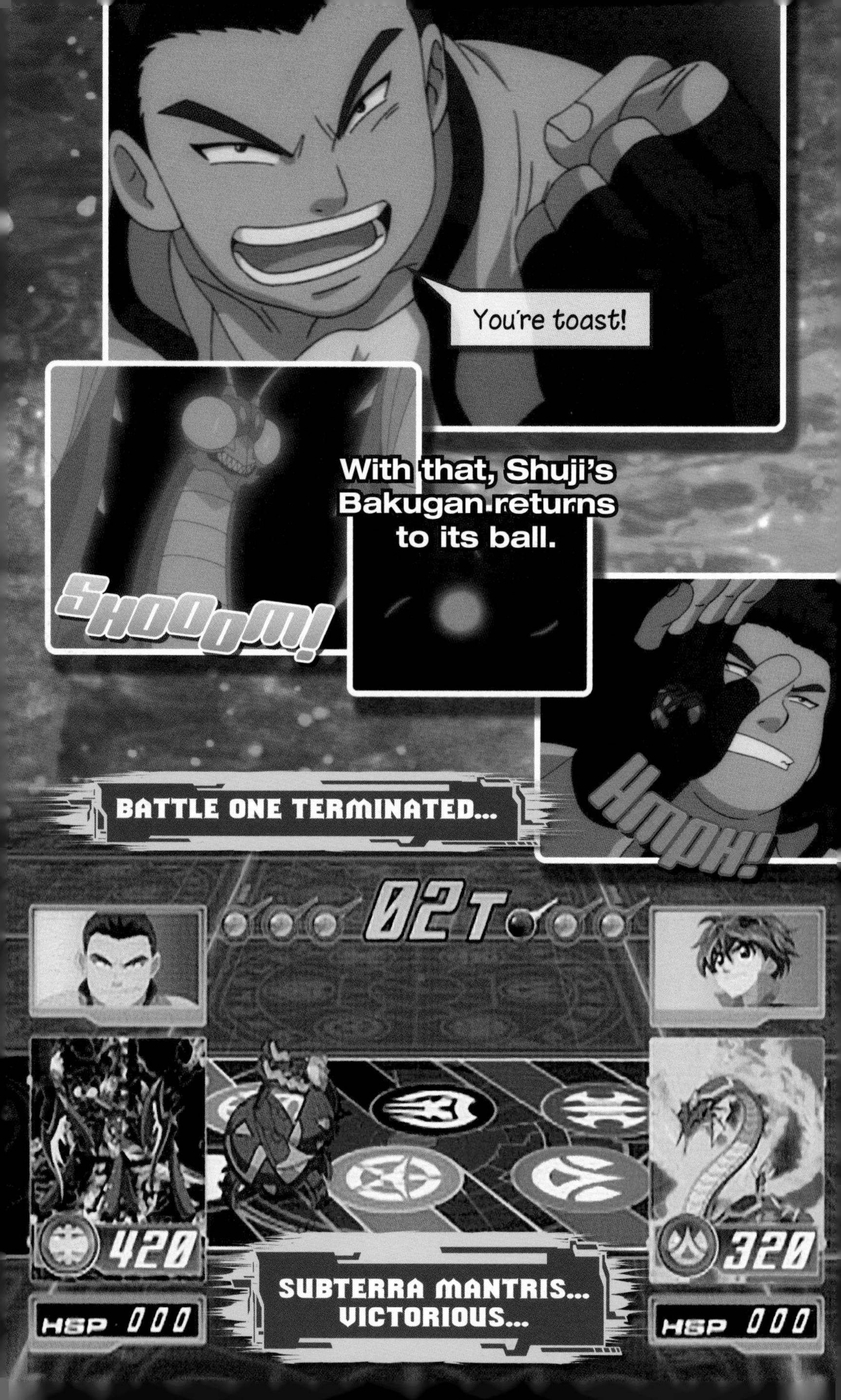
You're toast!
SHOOOM!
With that, Shuji's Bakugan returns to its ball.
HMPH!
BATTLE ONE TERMINATED...
02T
420
320
HSP 000
SUBTERRA MANTRIS... VICTORIOUS...
HSP 000

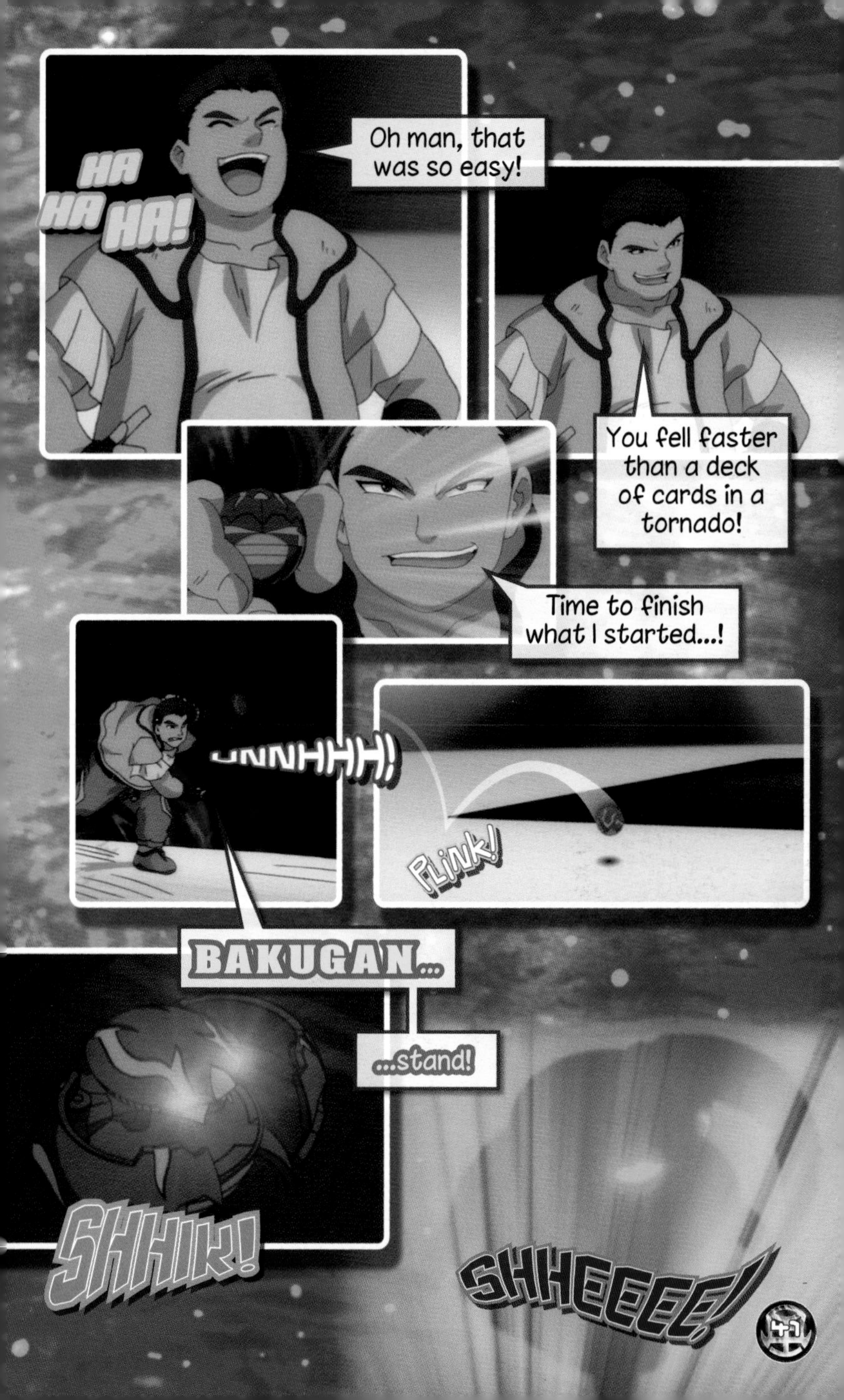

HA HA HA!
Oh man, that was so easy!
You fell faster than a deck of cards in a tornado!
Time to finish what I started...!
UNNHHH!
PLINK!
BAKUGAN...
...stand!
SHHIK!
SHHEEEE!

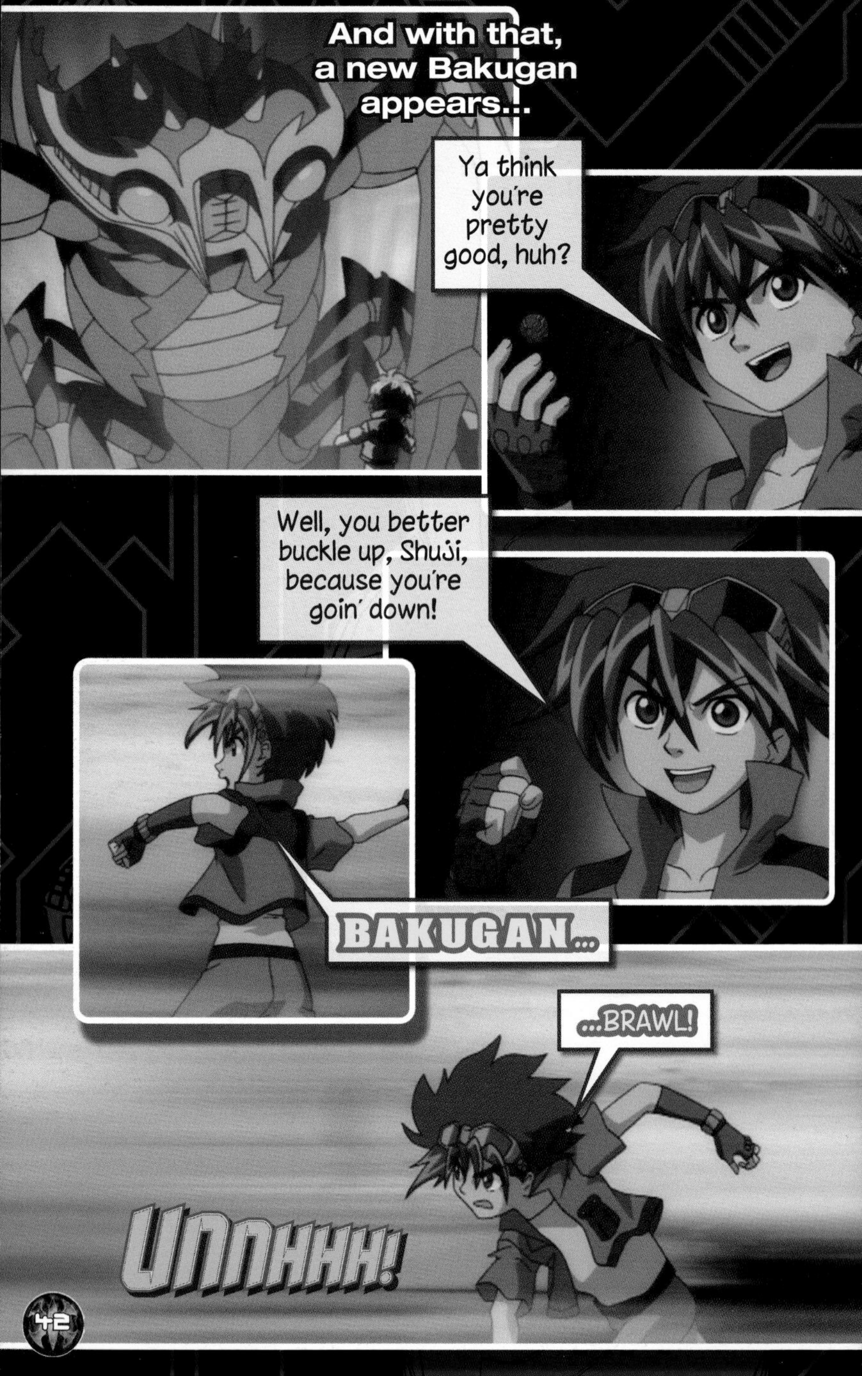

And with that, a new Bakugan appears...
Ya think you're pretty good, huh?
Well, you better buckle up, Shuji, because you're goin' down!
BAKUGAN...
...BRAWL!
UNNHHH!

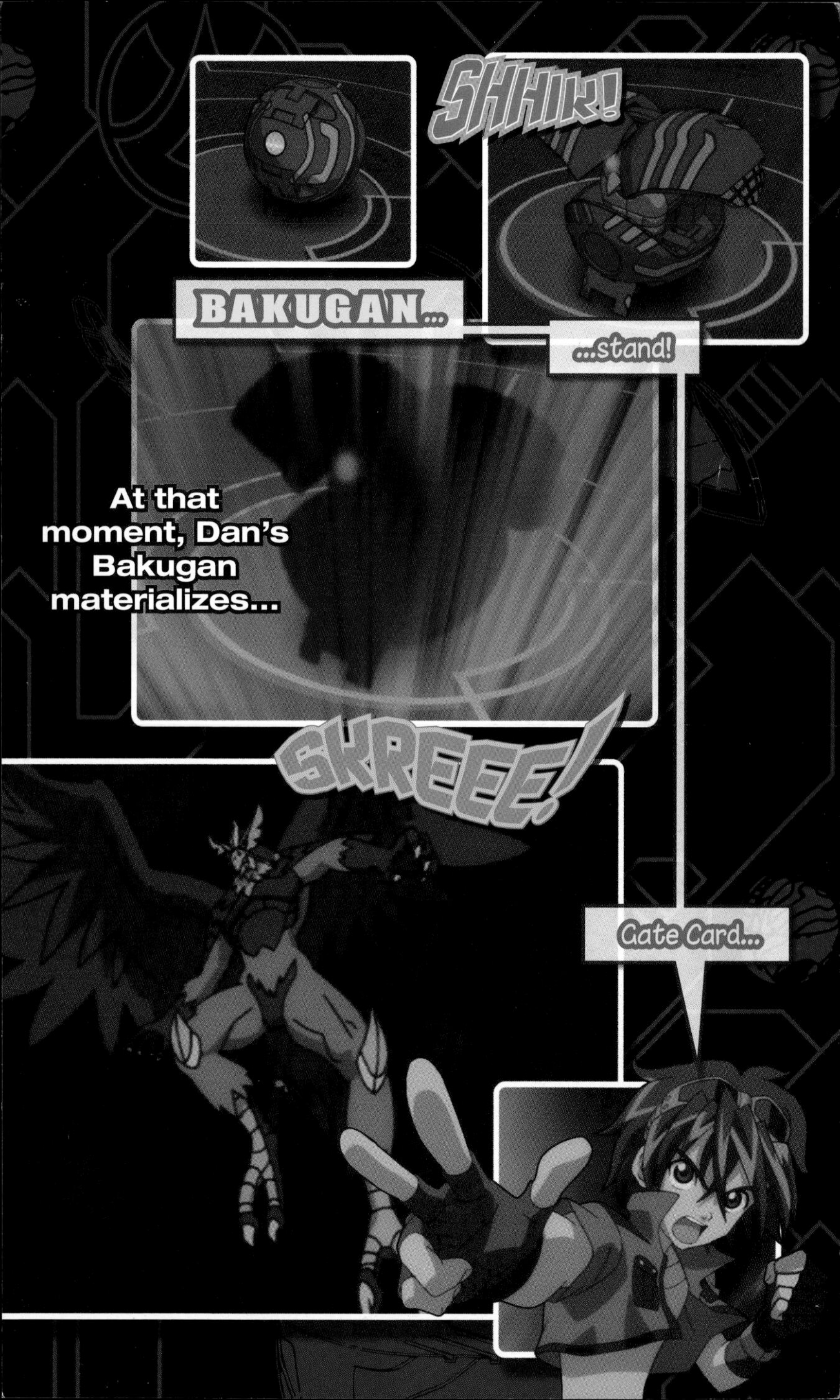

BAKUGAN...
SHHIK!
...stand!
At that moment, Dan's Bakugan materializes...
SKREEE!
Gate Card...

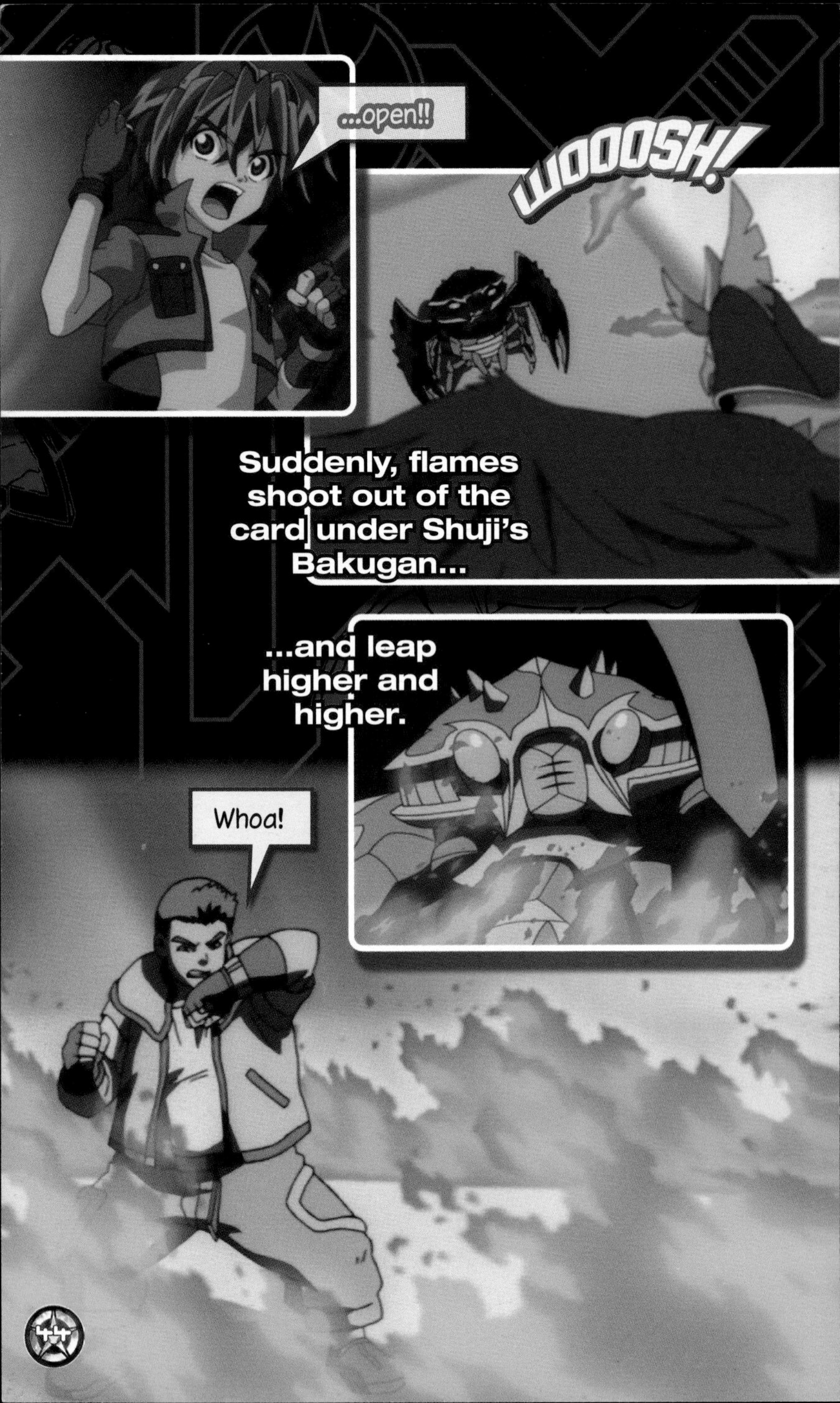
...open!!
WOOOSH!
Suddenly, flames shoot out of the card under Shuji's Bakugan...
...and leap higher and higher.
Whoa!

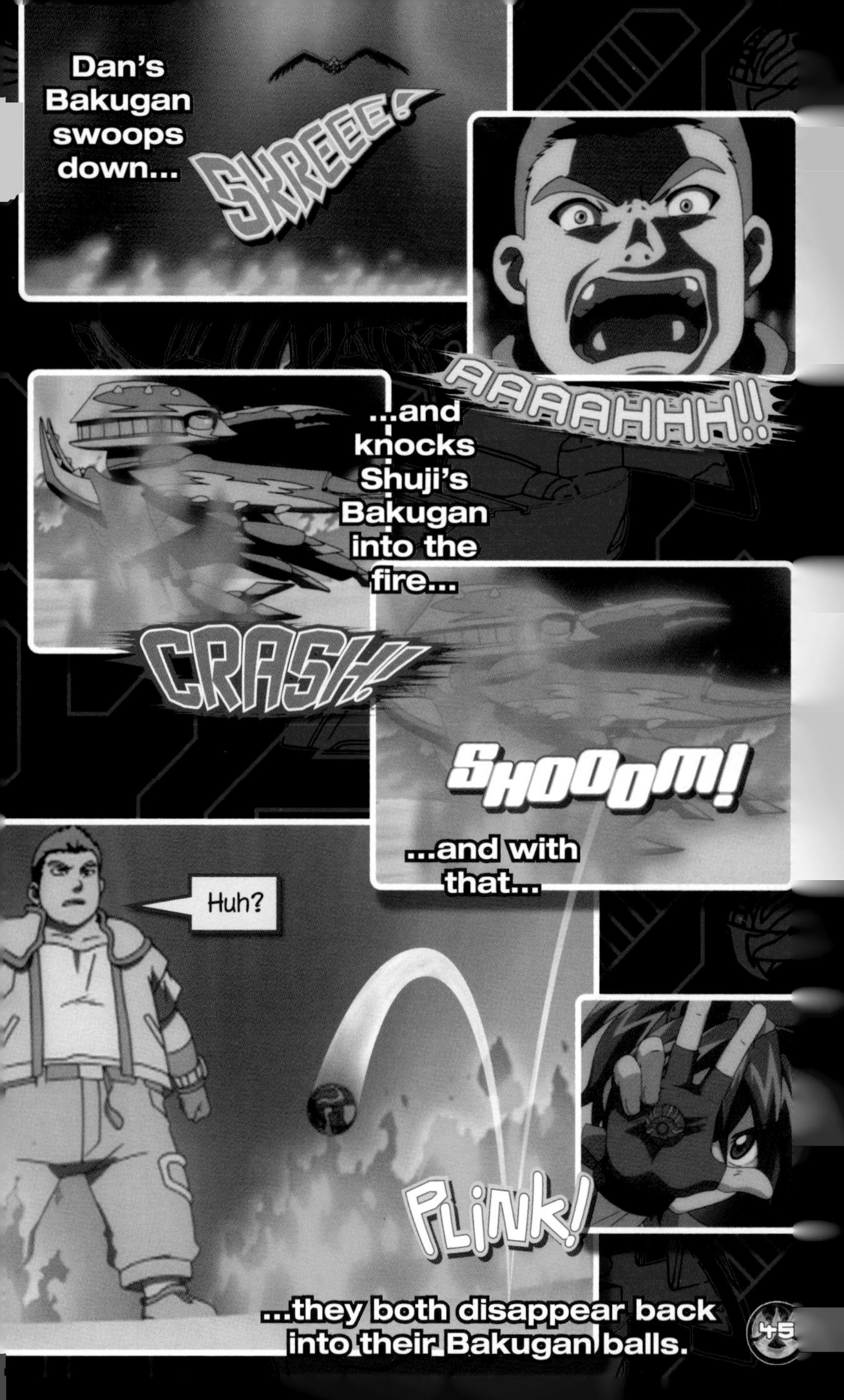
Dan's Bakugan swoops down...
SKREEE!
AAAAHHH!!
...and knocks Shuji's Bakugan into the fire...
CRASH!
SHOOOOM!
...and with that...
Huh?
PLINK!
...they both disappear back into their Bakugan balls.

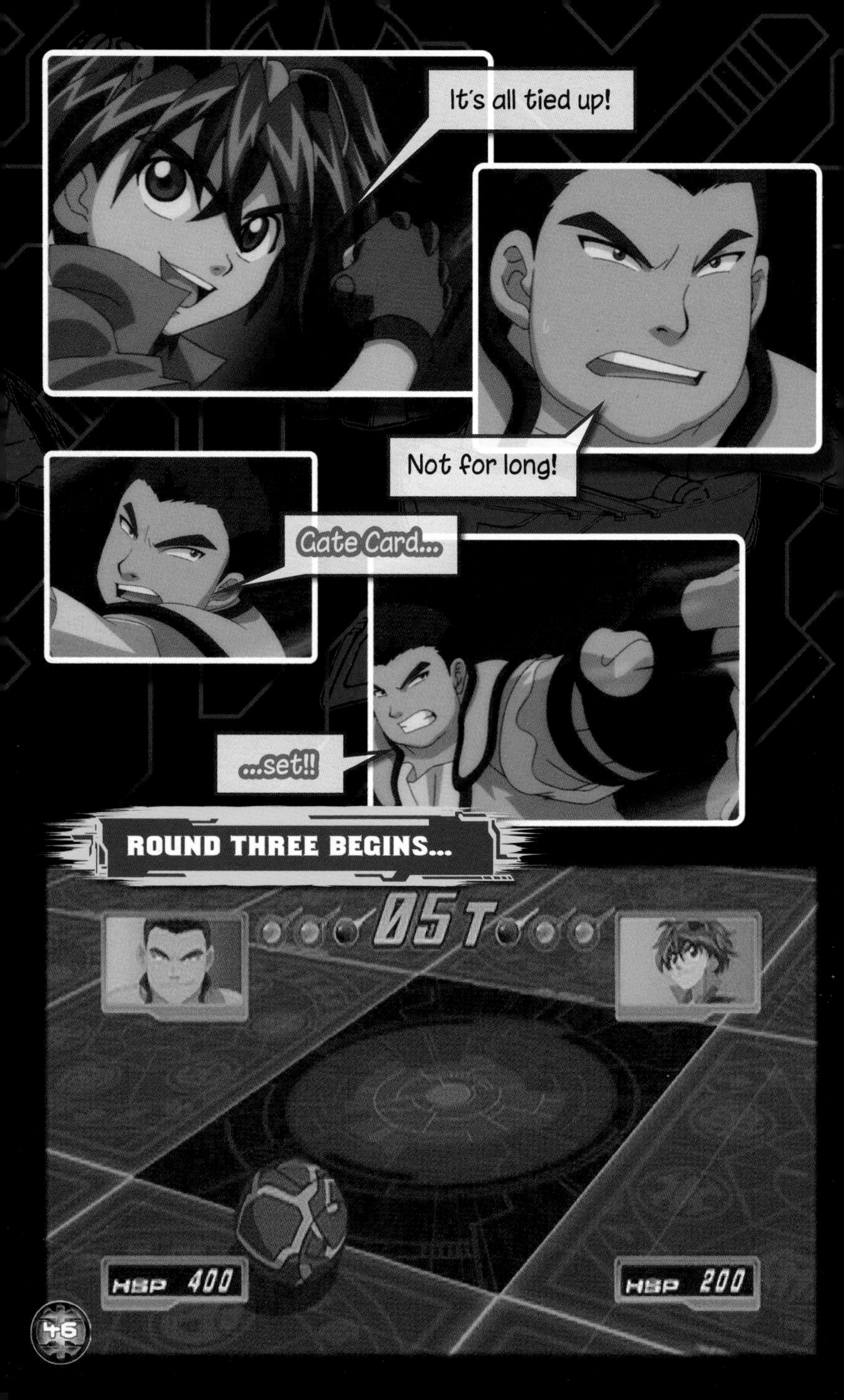
It's all tied up!
Not for long!
Gate Card...
...set!!
ROUND THREE BEGINS...
05 T
HSP 400
HSP 200

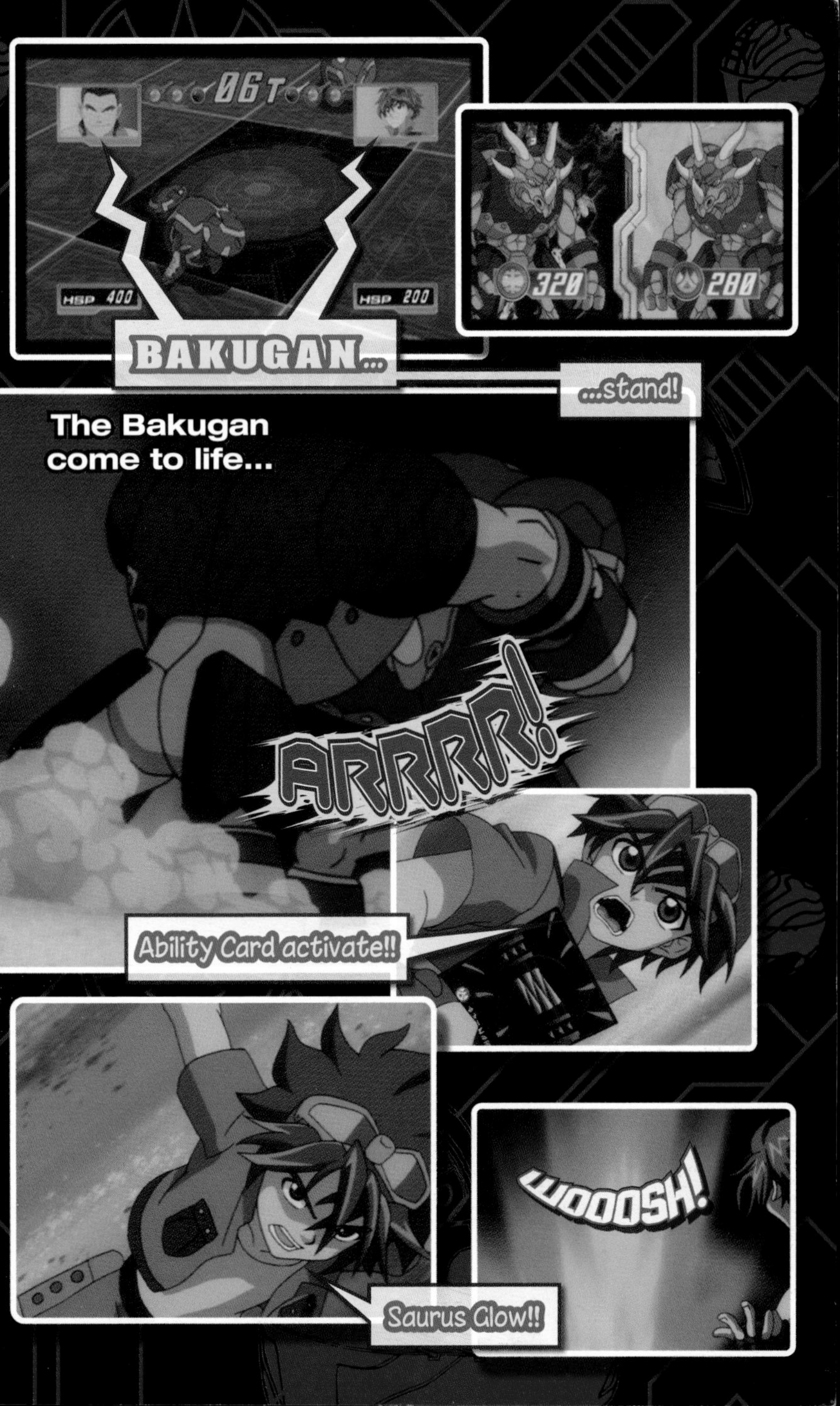
06T
HSP 400
HSP 200
BAKUGAN...
320
280
...stand!
The Bakugan come to life...
ARRRR!
Ability Card activate!!
Saurus Glow!!
WOOOSH!

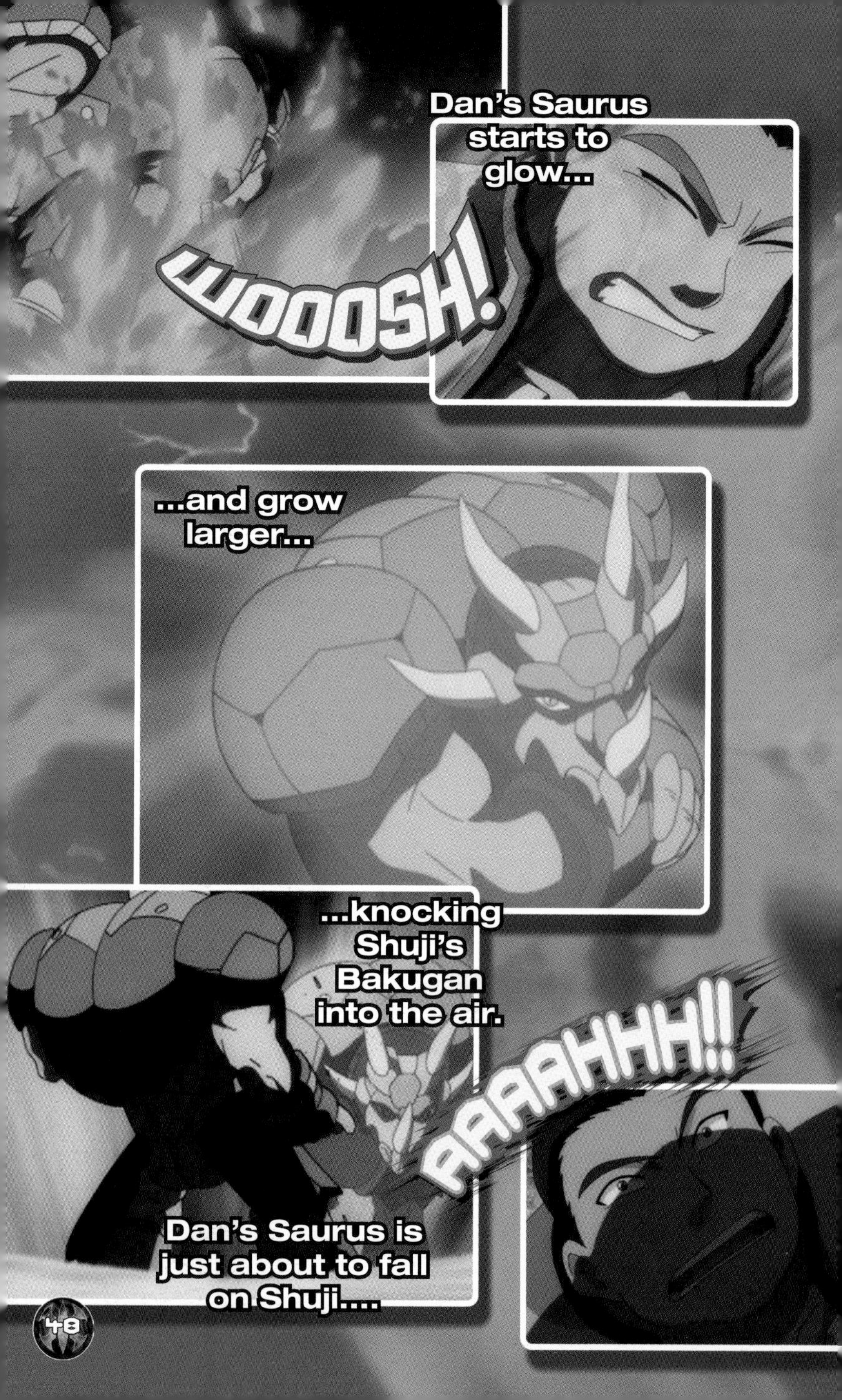
WOOOSH!
Dan's Saurus starts to glow...
...and grow larger...
...knocking Shuji's Bakugan into the air.
Dan's Saurus is just about to fall on Shuji....
AAAAHHH!!

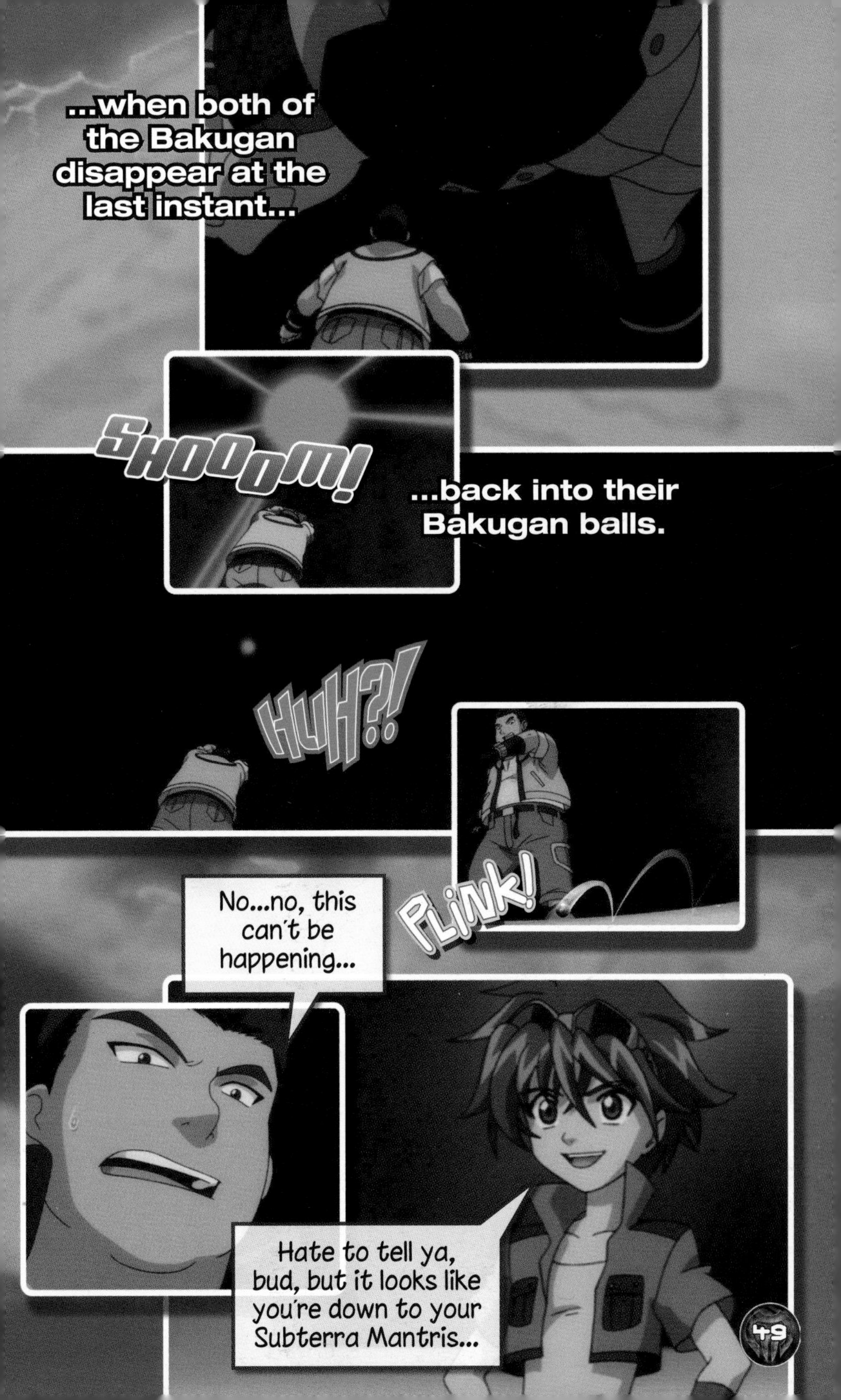

...when both of the Bakugan disappear at the last instant...
SHOOOOM!
...back into their Bakugan balls.
HUH?!
PLINK!
No...no, this can't be happening...
Hate to tell ya, bud, but it looks like you're down to your Subterra Mantris...

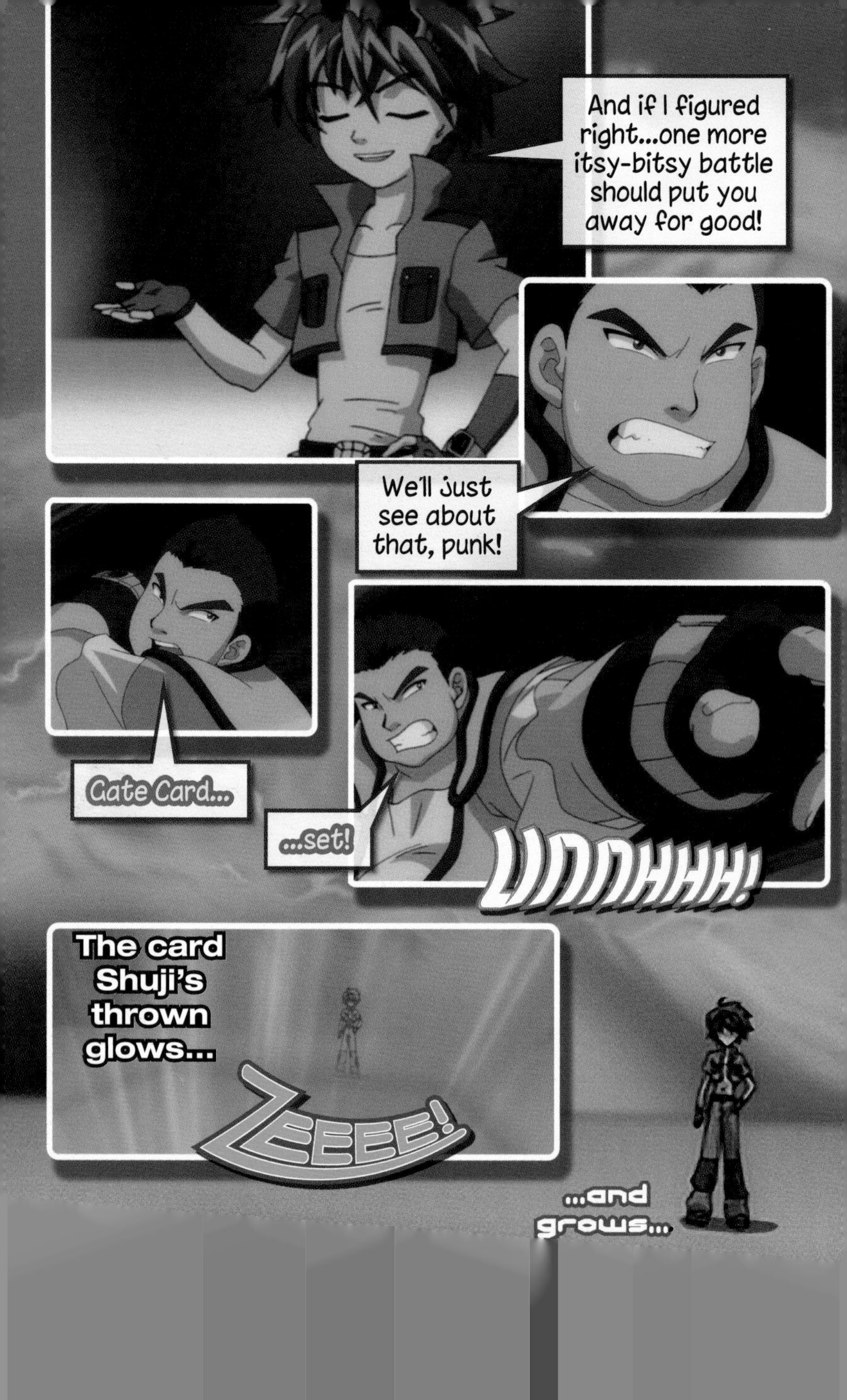
And if I figured right...one more itsy-bitsy battle should put you away for good!
We'll just see about that, punk!
Gate Card...
...set!
UNNHHH!
The card Shuji's thrown glows...
ZEEEE!
...and grows...

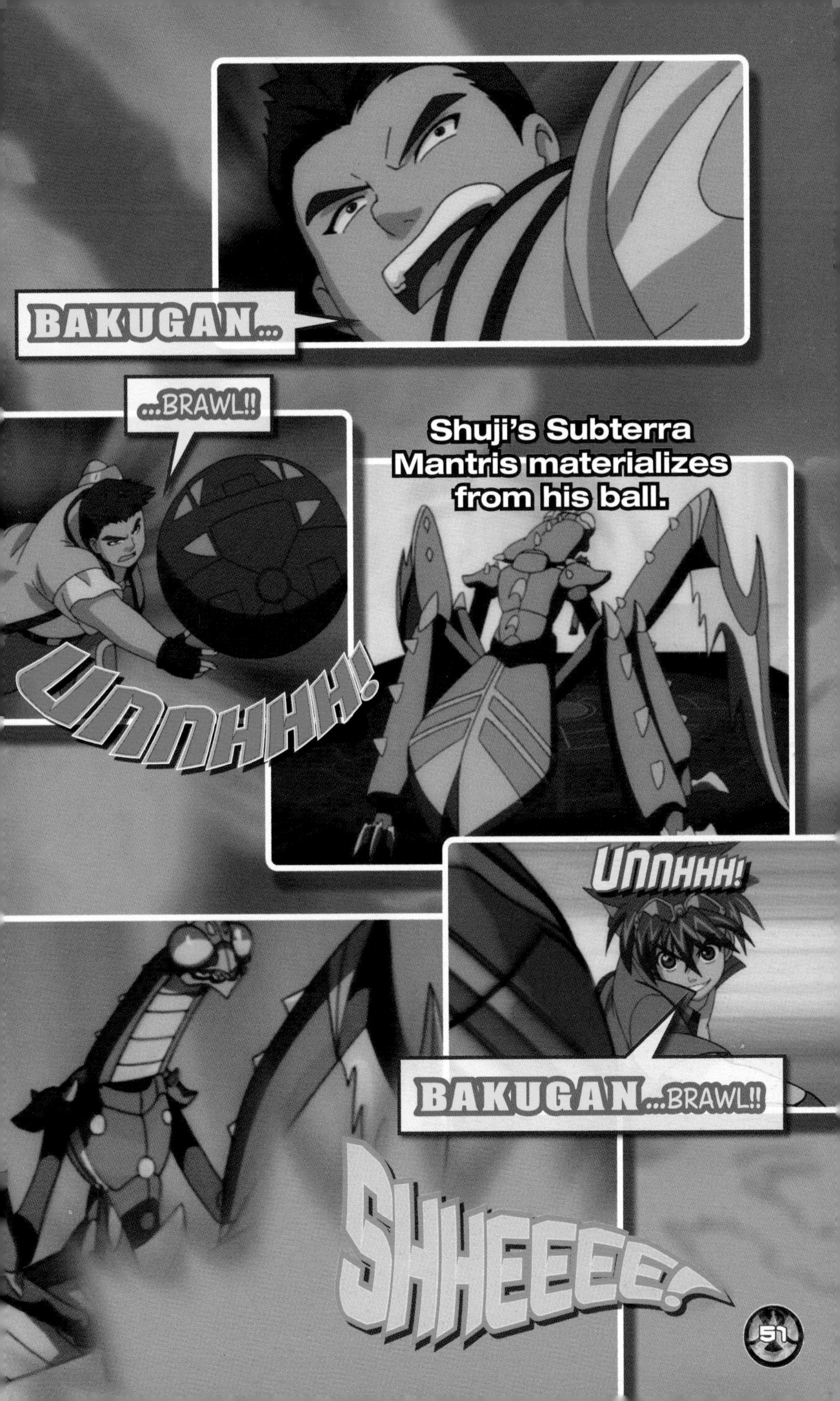
BAKUGAN...
...BRAWL!!
UNNHHH!
Shuji's Subterra Mantris materializes from his ball.
UNNHHH!
BAKUGAN...BRAWL!!
SHHEEEE!

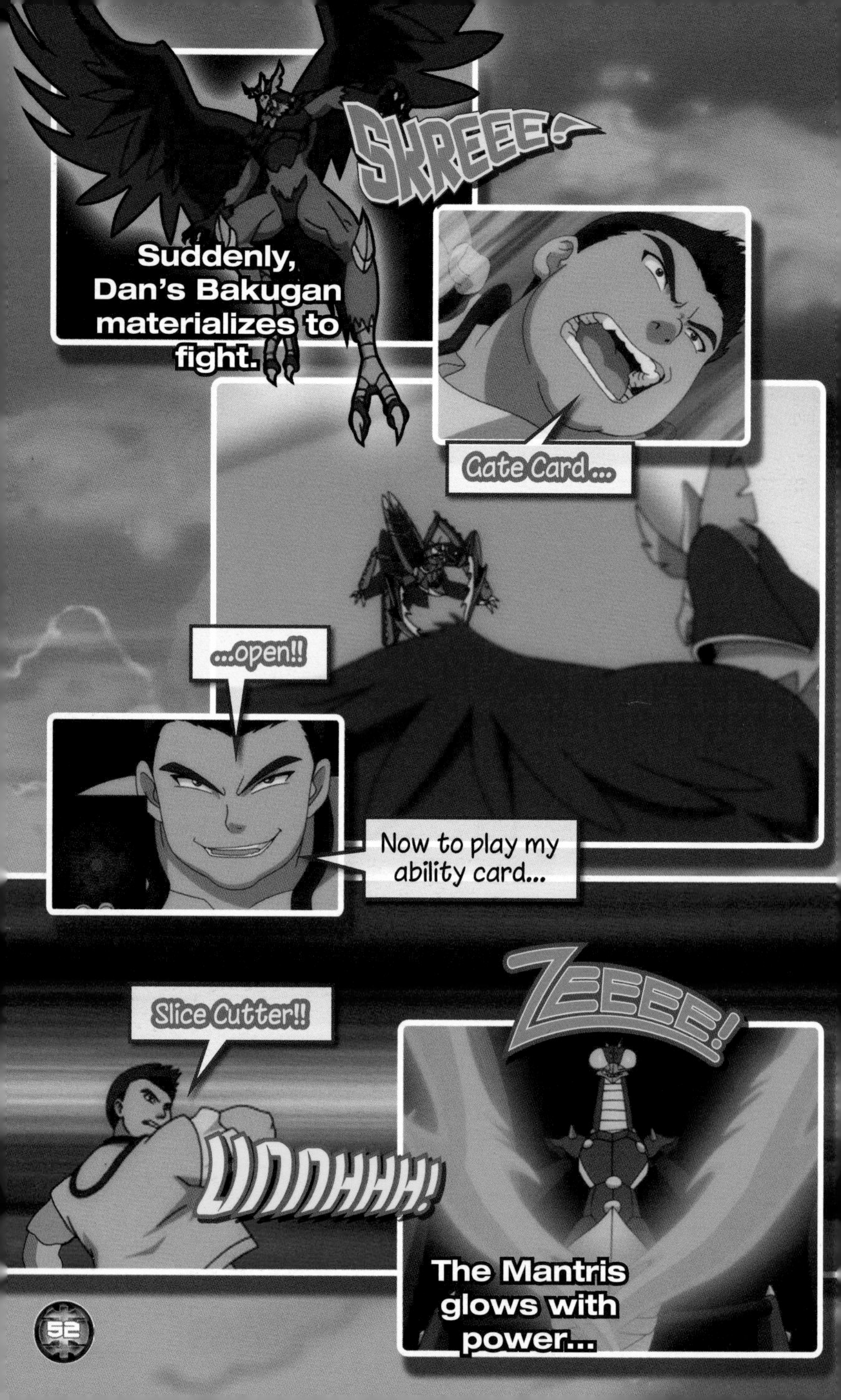
SKREEE!
Suddenly, Dan's Bakugan materializes to fight.
Gate Card...
...open!!
Now to play my ability card...
Slice Cutter!!
UNNHHH!
ZEEEE!
The Mantris glows with power...

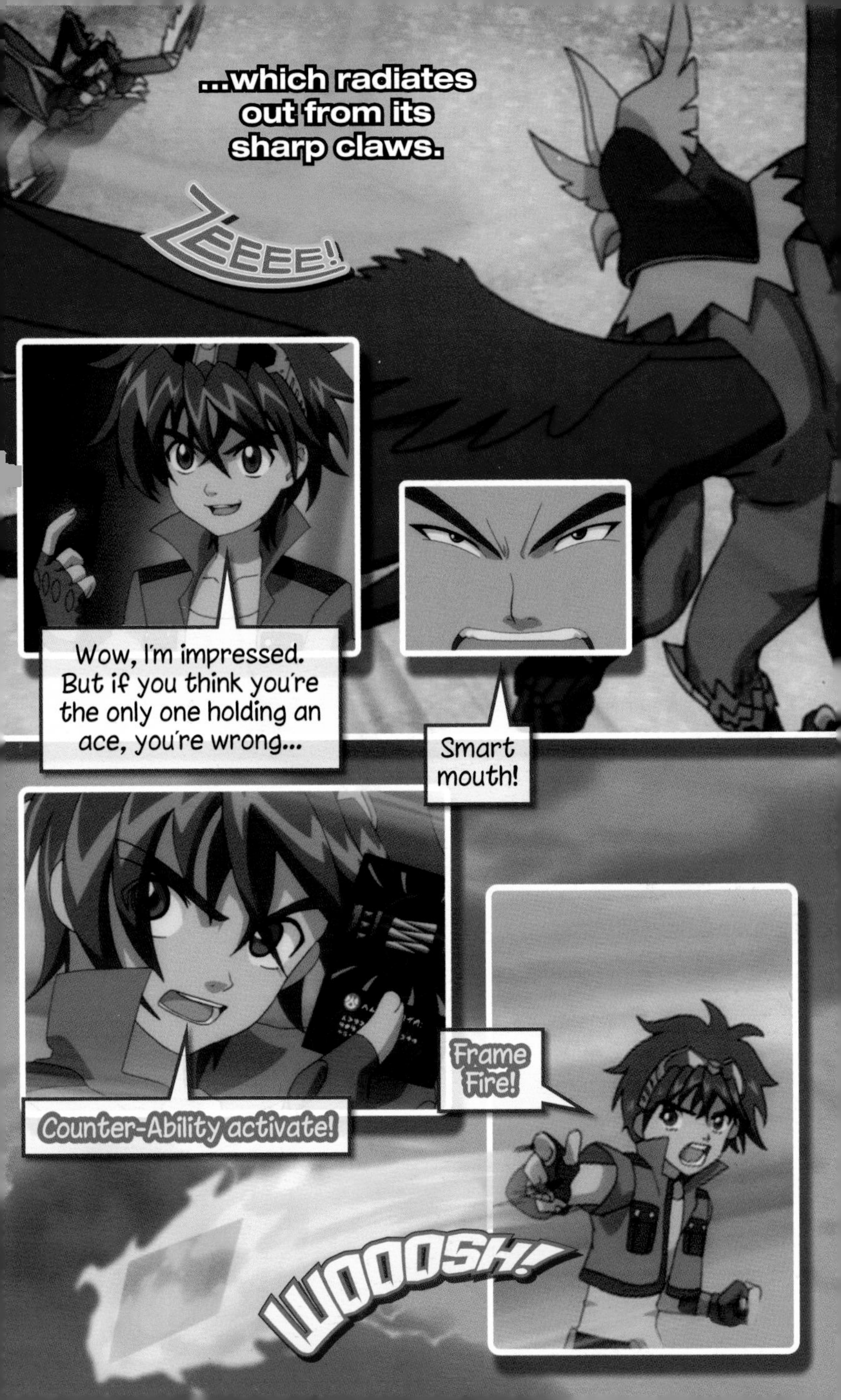
...which radiates out from its sharp claws.
ZEEEEE!
Wow, I'm impressed. But if you think you're the only one holding an ace, you're wrong...
Smart mouth!
Counter-Ability activate!
Frame Fire!
WOOOSH!

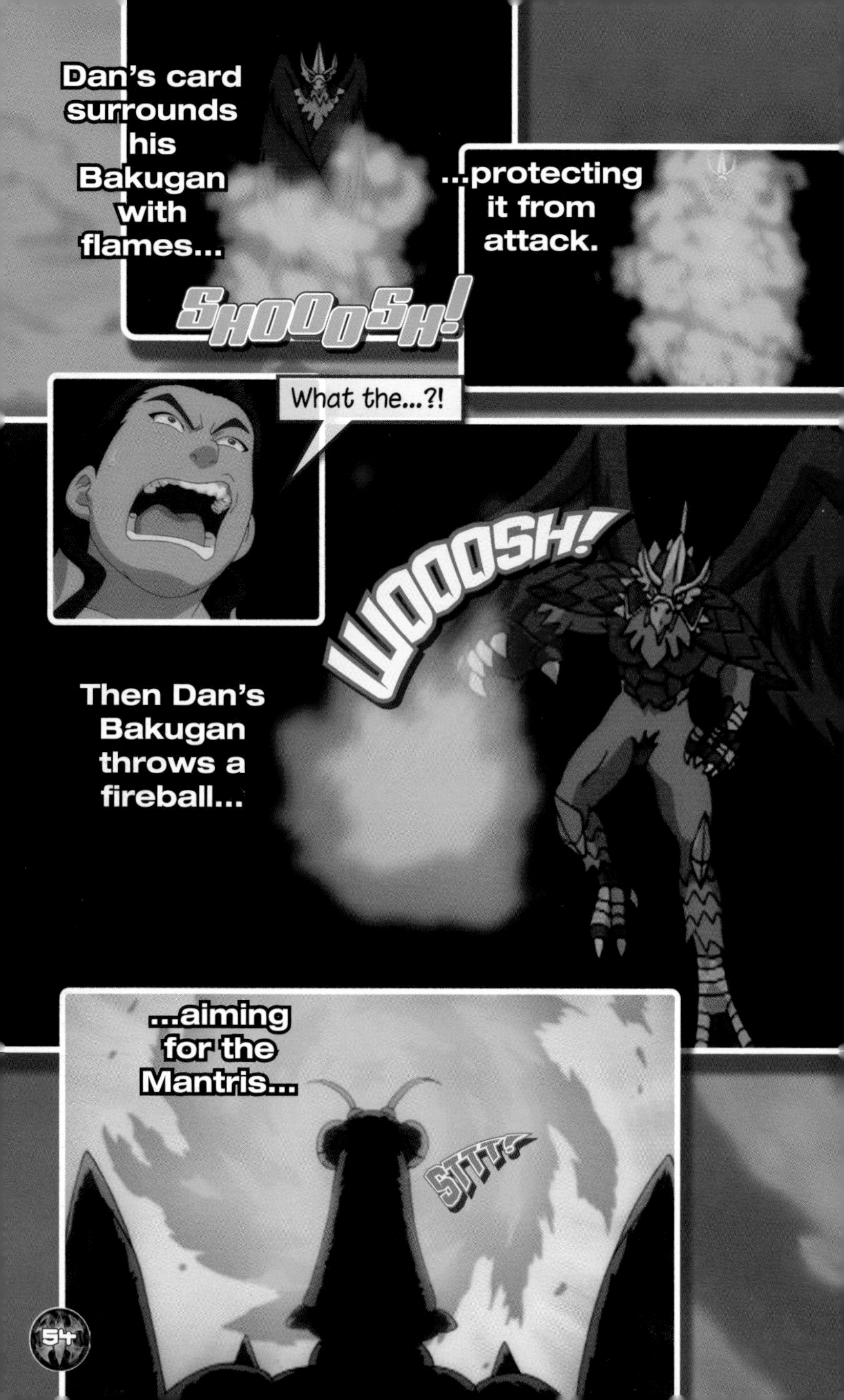
Dan's card surrounds his Bakugan with flames...
SHOOOOSH!
...protecting it from attack.
What the...?!
WOOOSH!
Then Dan's Bakugan throws a fireball...
...aiming for the Mantris...

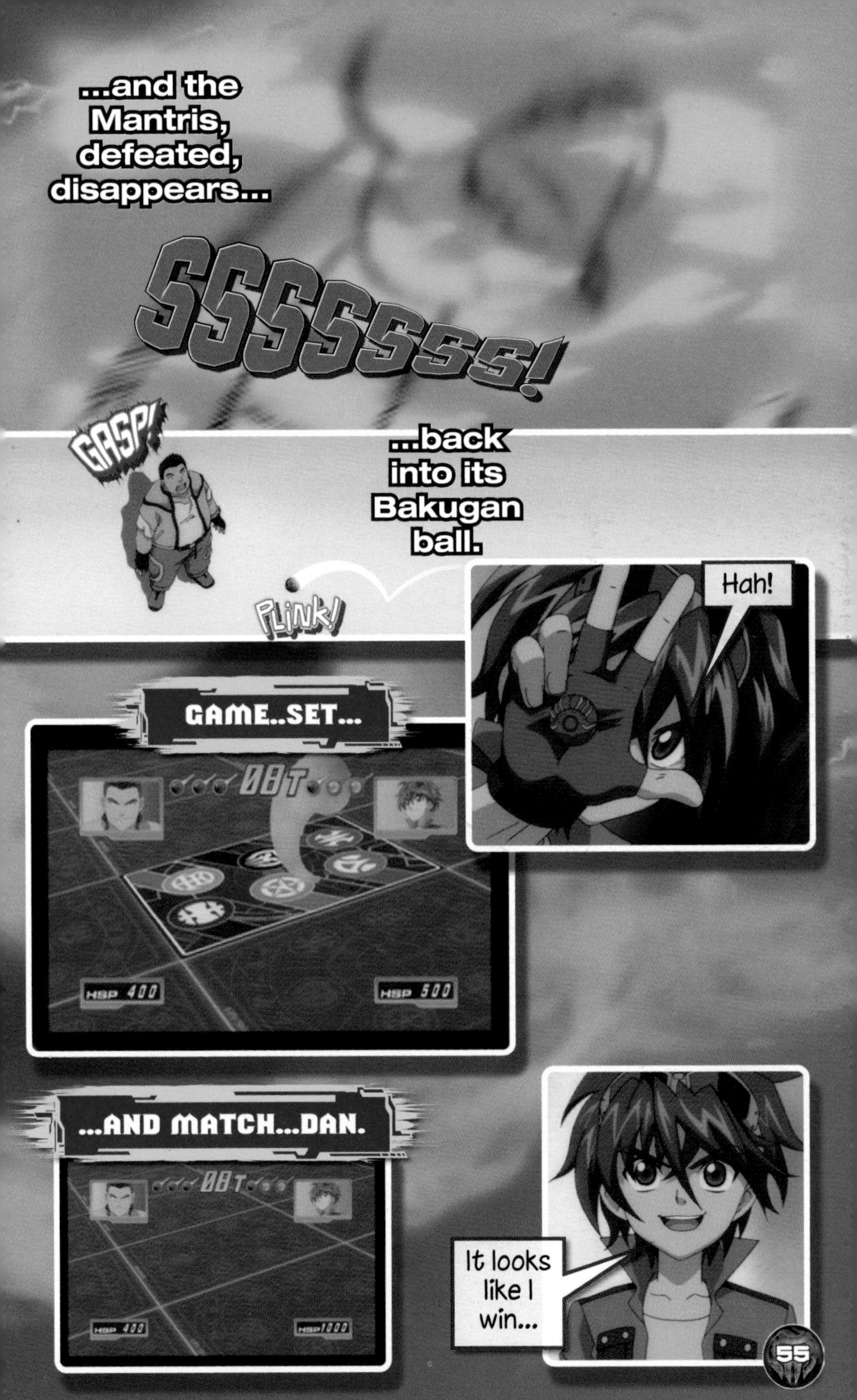

...and the Mantris, defeated, disappears...
SSSSSSS!
GASP!
...back into its Bakugan ball.
PLINK!
Hah!
GAME..SET...
HSP 400
HSP 500
...AND MATCH...DAN.
HSP 400
HSP 1000
It looks like I win...

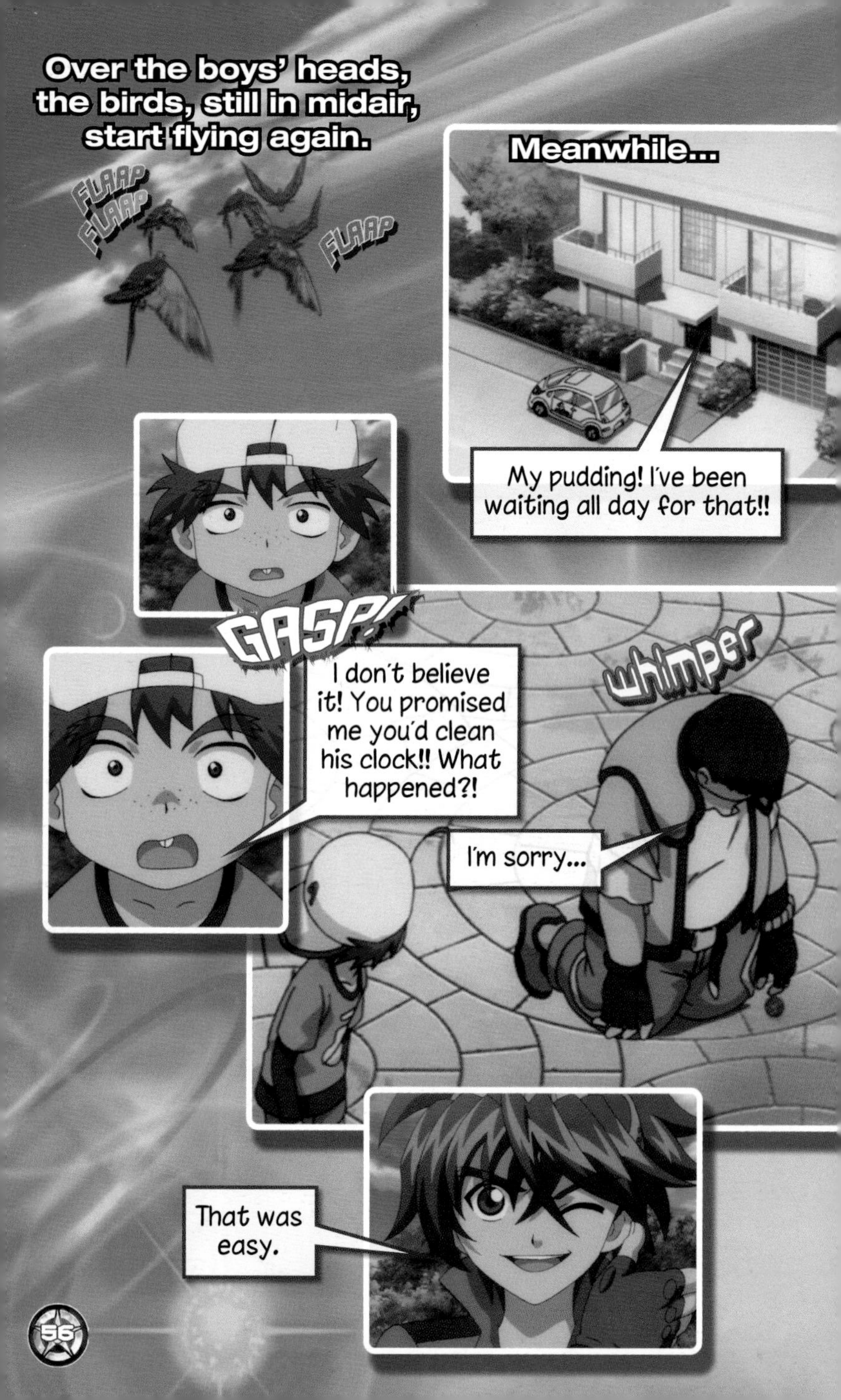
Over the boys' heads, the birds, still in midair, start flying again.
FLAAP
FLAAP
FLAAP
Meanwhile...
My pudding! I've been waiting all day for that!!
GASP!
I don't believe it! You promised me you'd clean his clock!! What happened?!
whimper
I'm sorry...
That was easy.

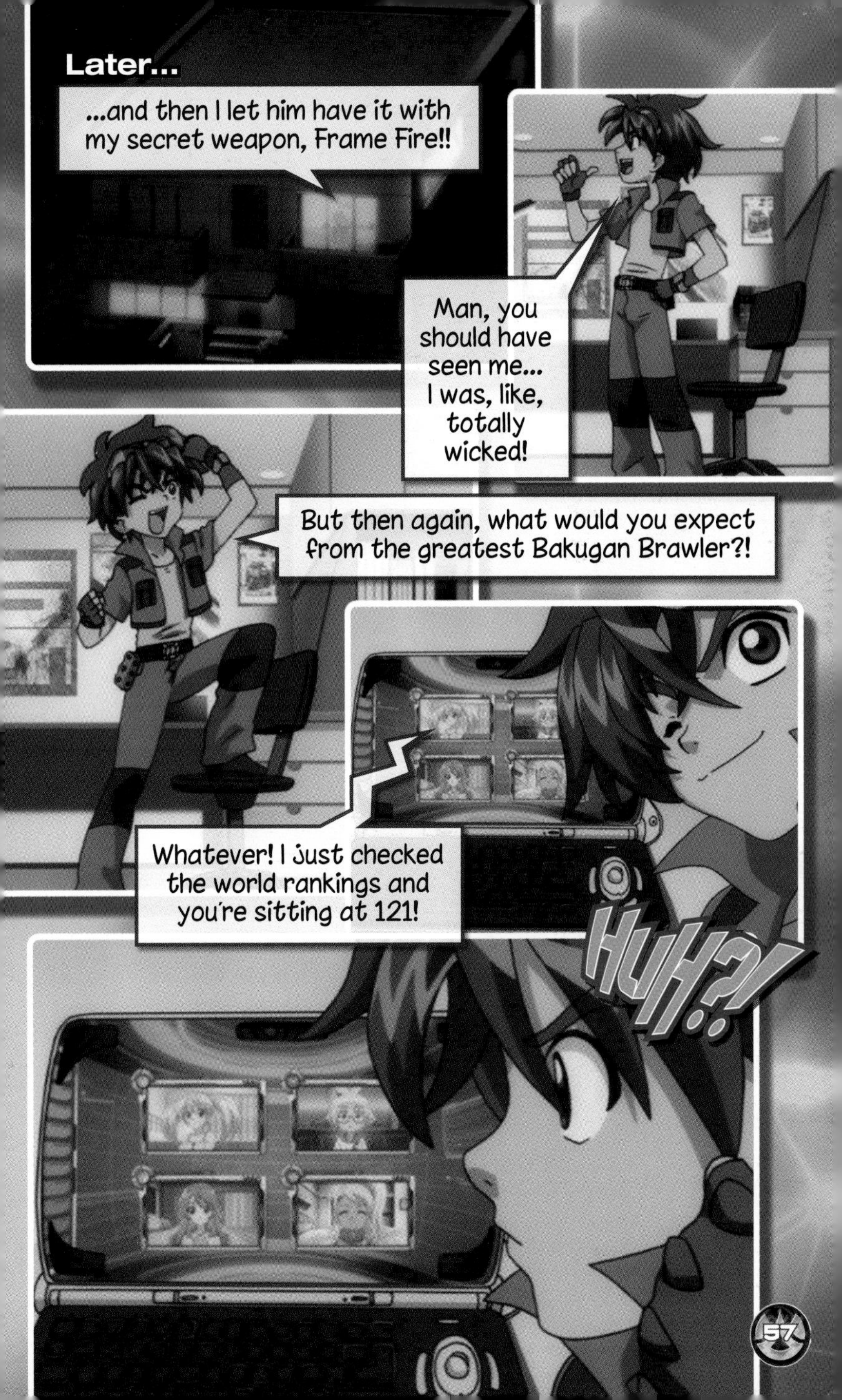

Later...
...and then I let him have it with my secret weapon, Frame Fire!!
Man, you should have seen me... I was, like, totally wicked!
But then again, what would you expect from the greatest Bakugan Brawler?!
Whatever! I just checked the world rankings and you're sitting at 121!
HUH?!

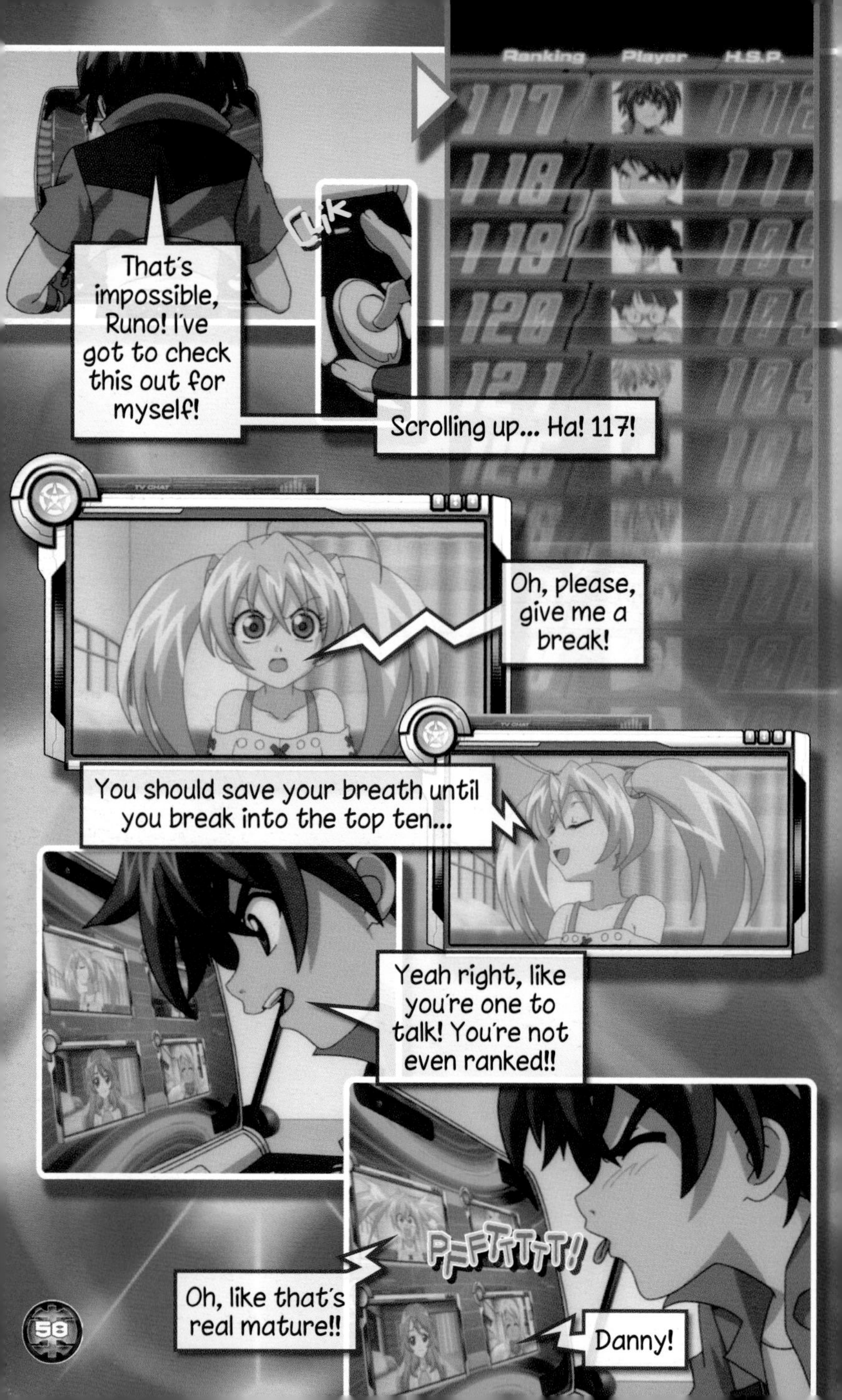
Ranking Player H.S.P.
That's impossible, Runo! I've got to check this out for myself!
CLIK
Scrolling up... Ha! 117!
Oh, please, give me a break!
You should save your breath until you break into the top ten...
Yeah right, like you're one to talk! You're not even ranked!!
PFFTTTTT!
Oh, like that's real mature!!
Danny!

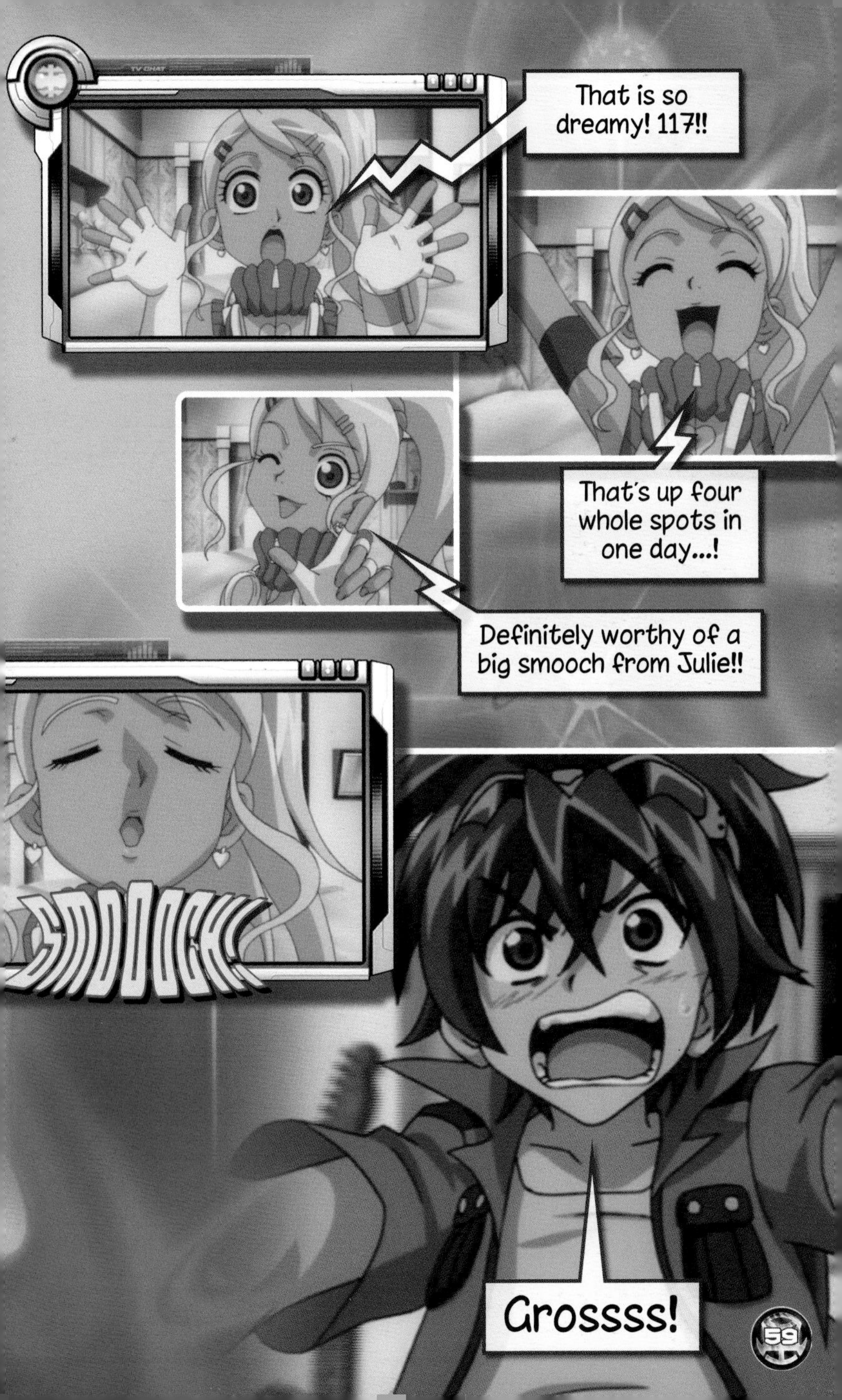
That is so dreamy! 117!!
That's up four whole spots in one day...!
Definitely worthy of a big smooch from Julie!!
SMOOCH
Grossss!

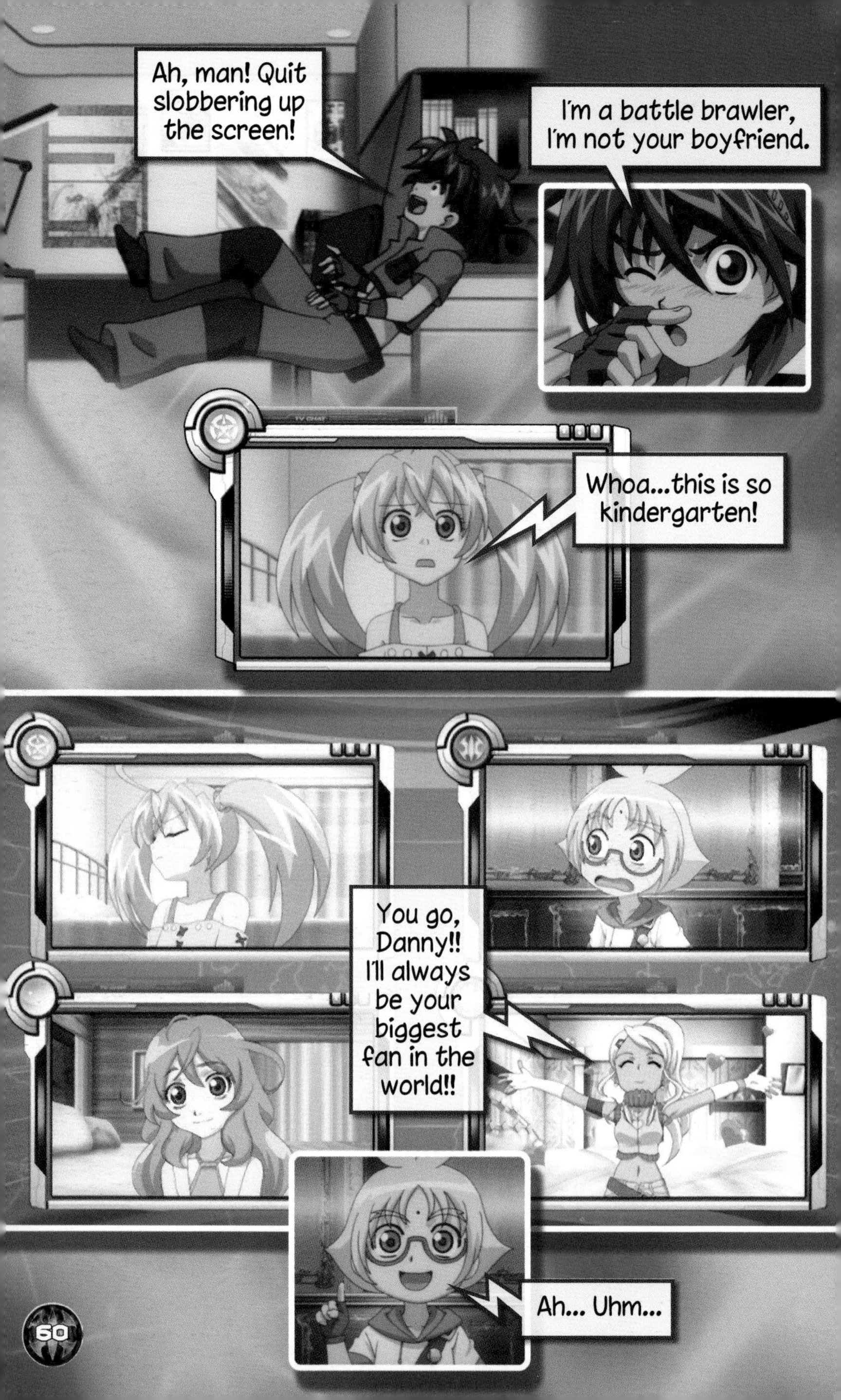

Ah, man! Quit slobbering up the screen!
I'm a battle brawler, I'm not your boyfriend.
Whoa...this is so kindergarten!
You go, Danny!! I'll always be your biggest fan in the world!!
Ah... Uhm...

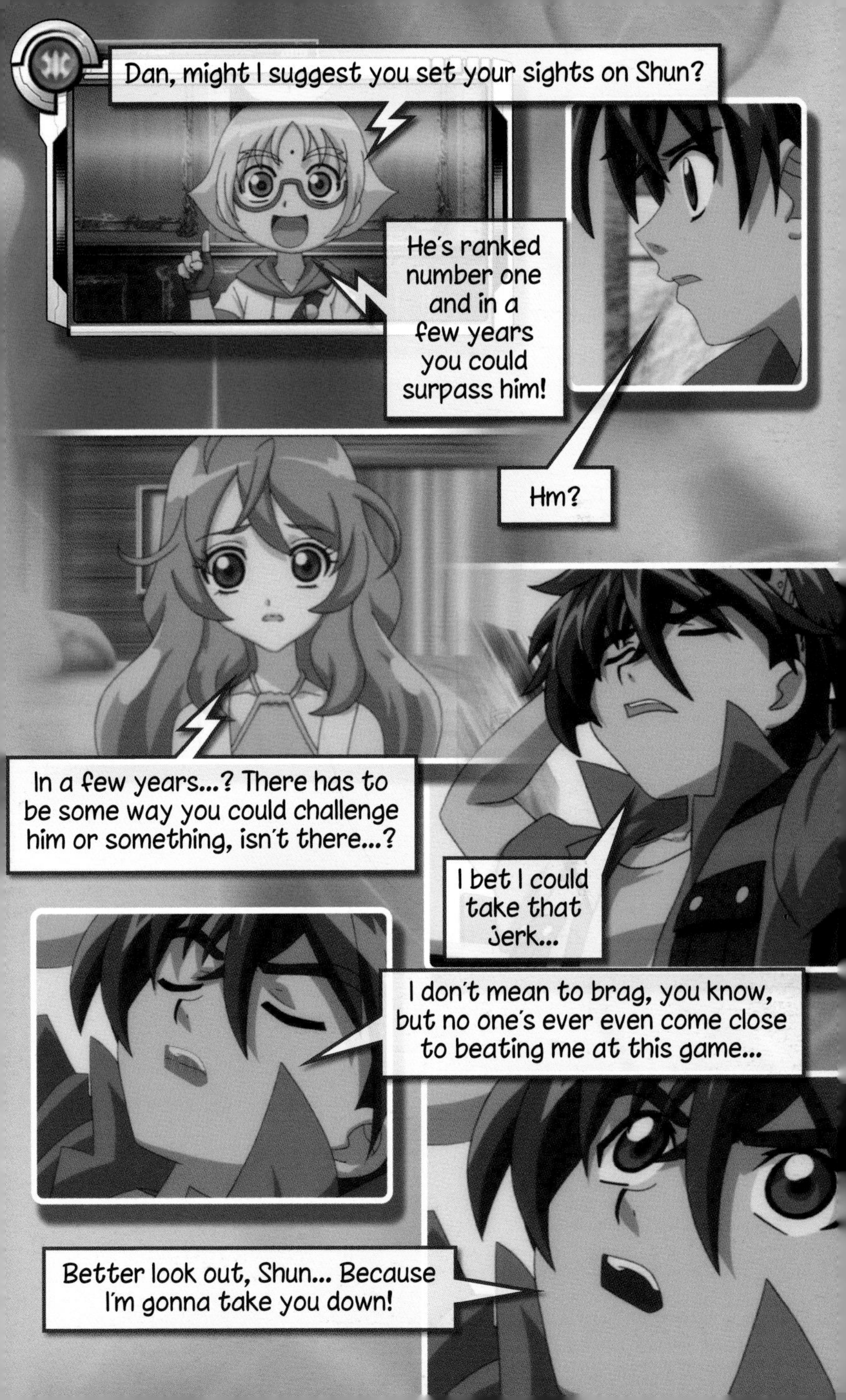
Dan, might I suggest you set your sights on Shun?
He's ranked number one and in a few years you could surpass him!
Hm?
In a few years...? There has to be some way you could challenge him or something, isn't there...?
I bet I could take that jerk...
I don't mean to brag, you know, but no one's ever even come close to beating me at this game...
Better look out, Shun... Because I'm gonna take you down!

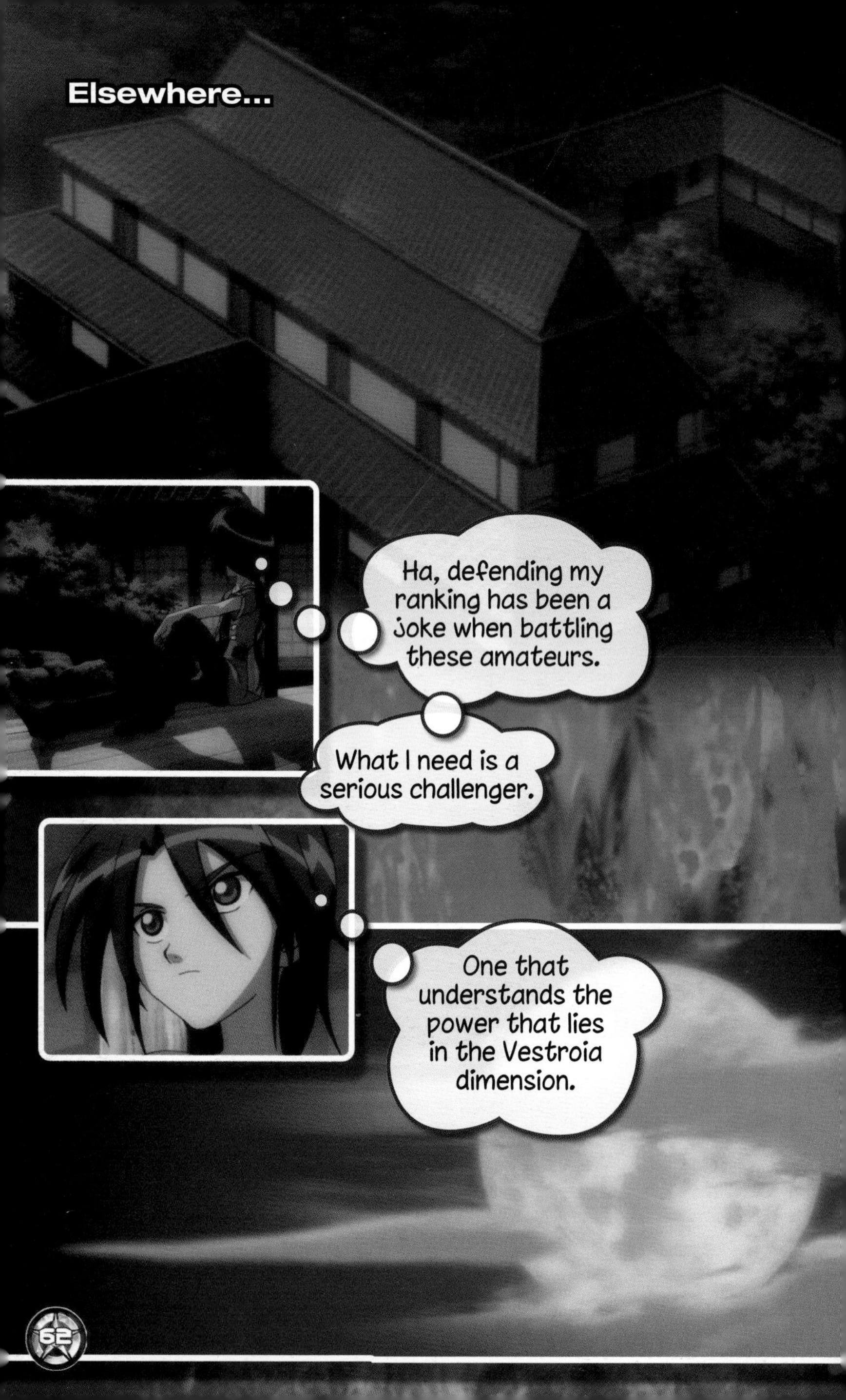
Elsewhere...
Ha, defending my ranking has been a joke when battling these amateurs.
What I need is a serious challenger.
One that understands the power that lies in the Vestroia dimension.

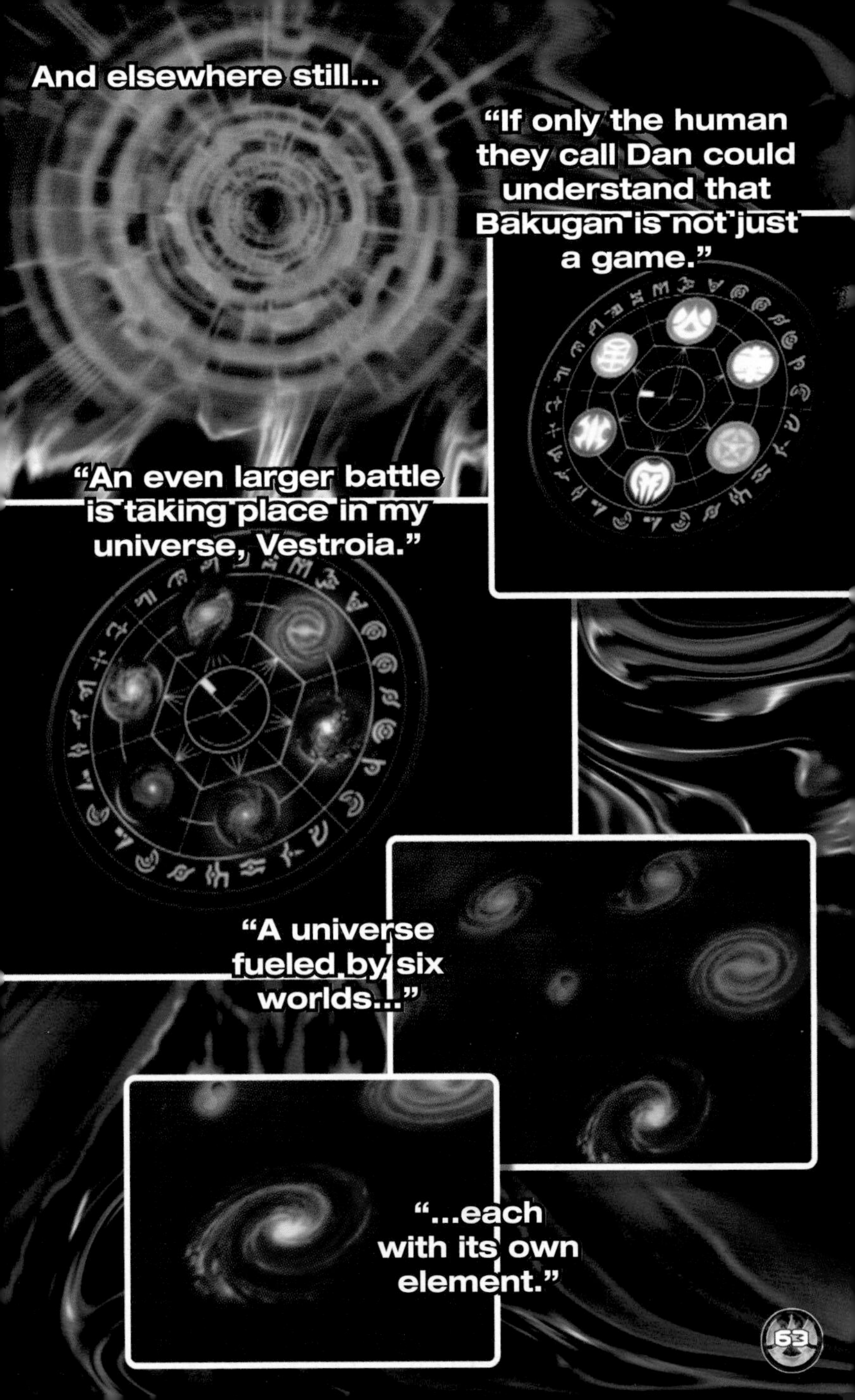
And elsewhere still...
"If only the human they call Dan could understand that Bakugan is not just a game."
"An even larger battle is taking place in my universe, Vestroia."
"A universe fueled by six worlds..."
"...each with its own element."

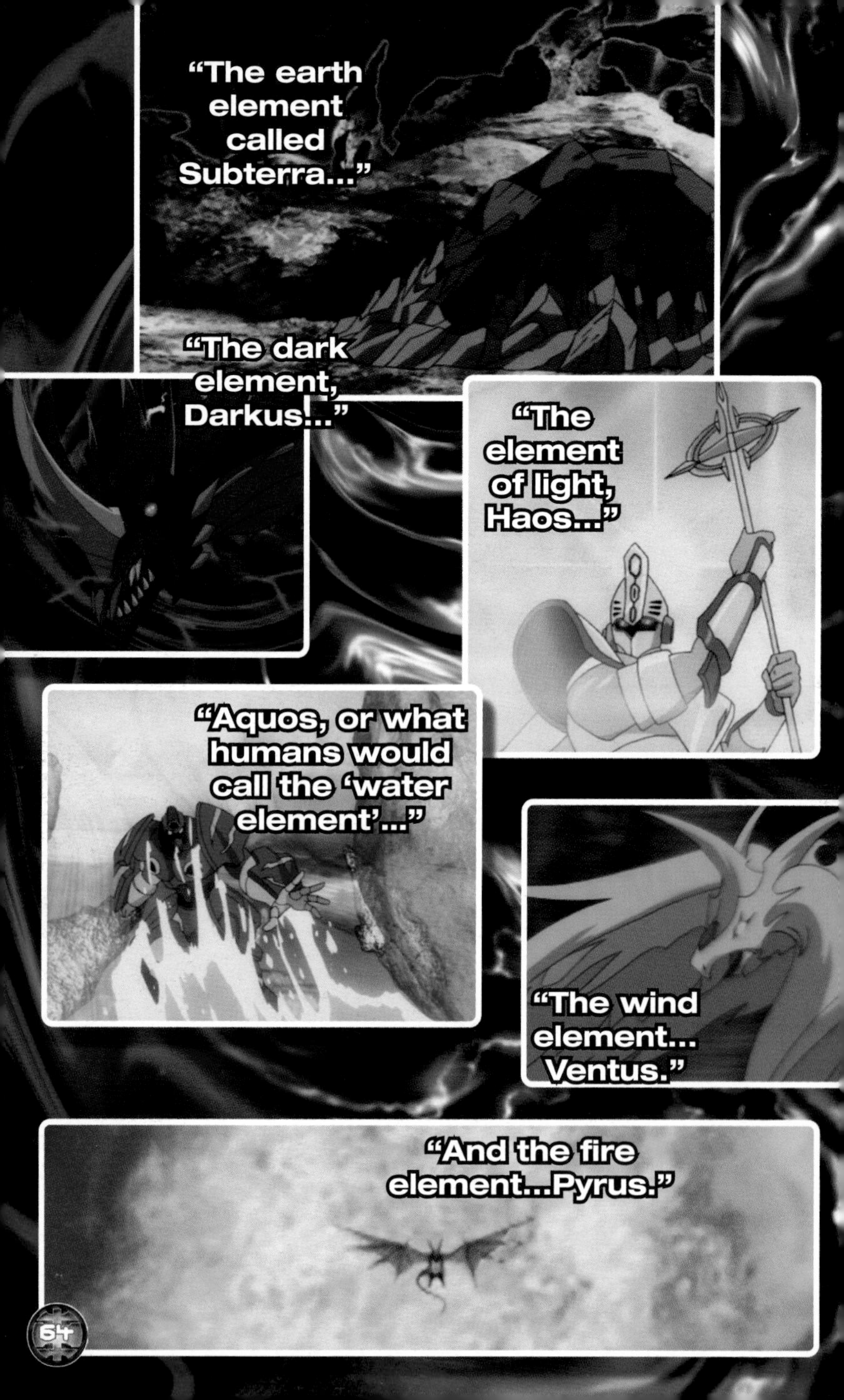
"The earth element called Subterra..."
"The dark element, Darkus!..."
"The element of light, Haos..."
"Aquos, or what humans would call the 'water element'..."
"The wind element... Ventus."
"And the fire element...Pyrus."

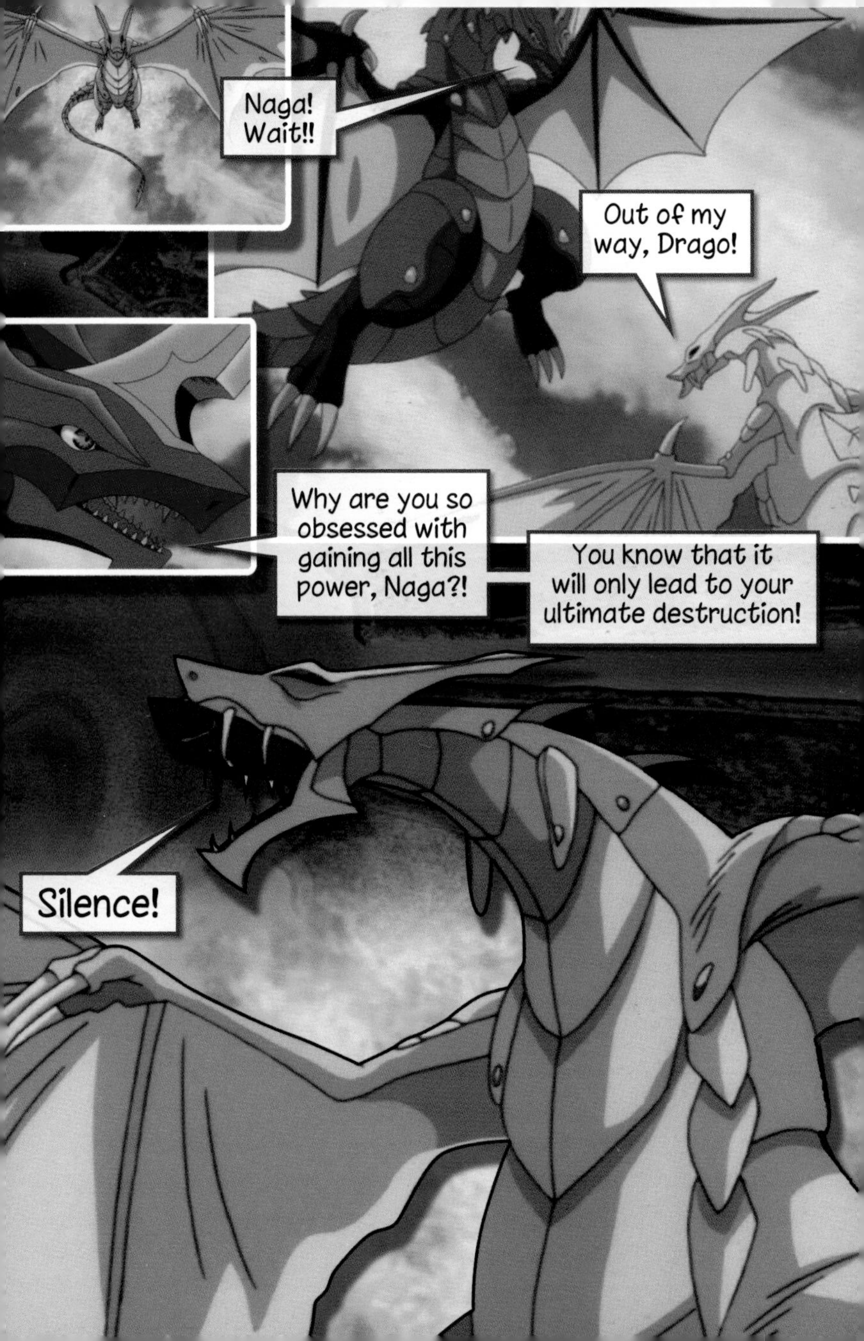
Naga! Wait!!
Out of my way, Drago!
Why are you so obsessed with gaining all this power, Naga?!
You know that it will only lead to your ultimate destruction!
Silence!

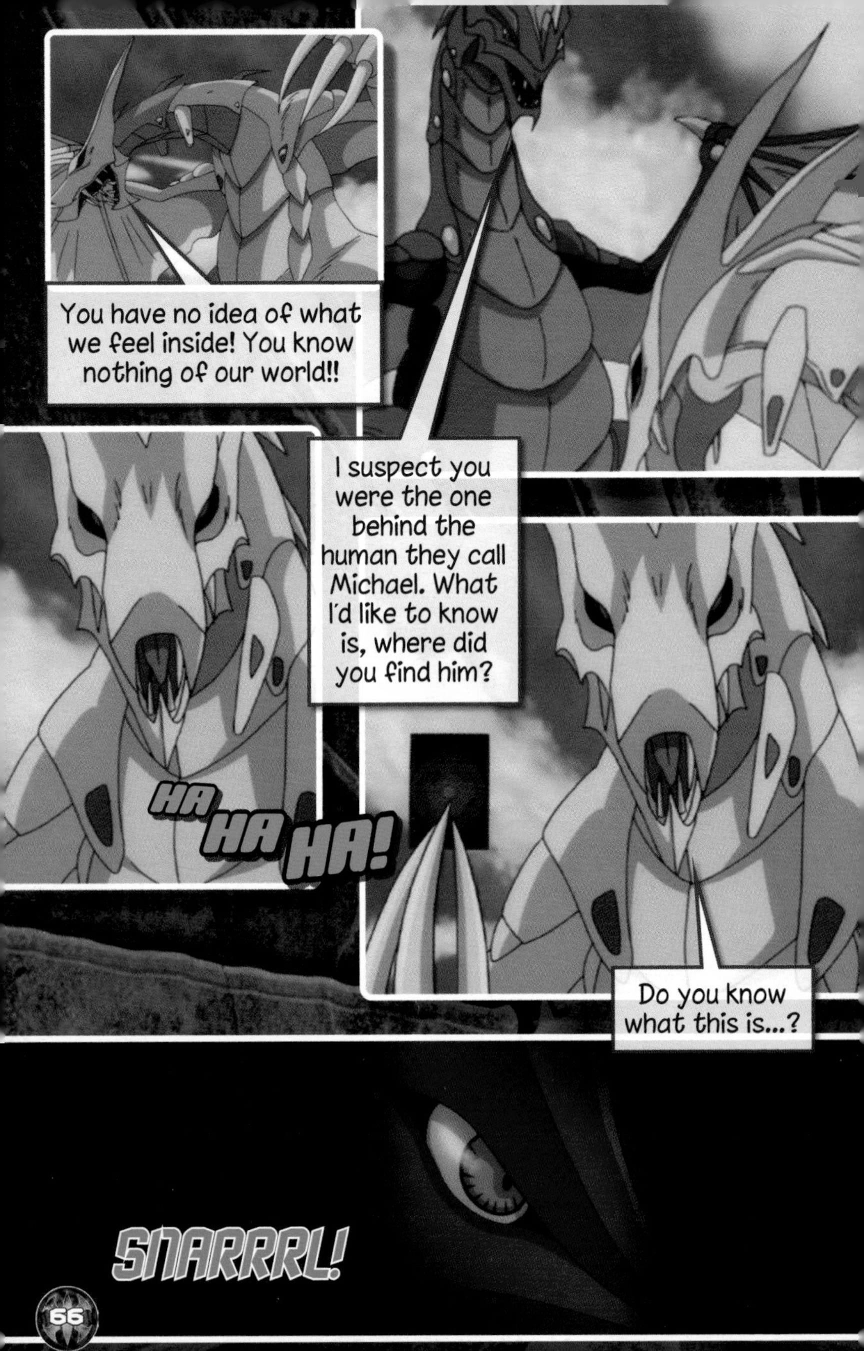
You have no idea of what we feel inside! You know nothing of our world!!
I suspect you were the one behind the human they call Michael. What I'd like to know is, where did you find him?
HA HA HA!
Do you know what this is...?
SNARRRL!

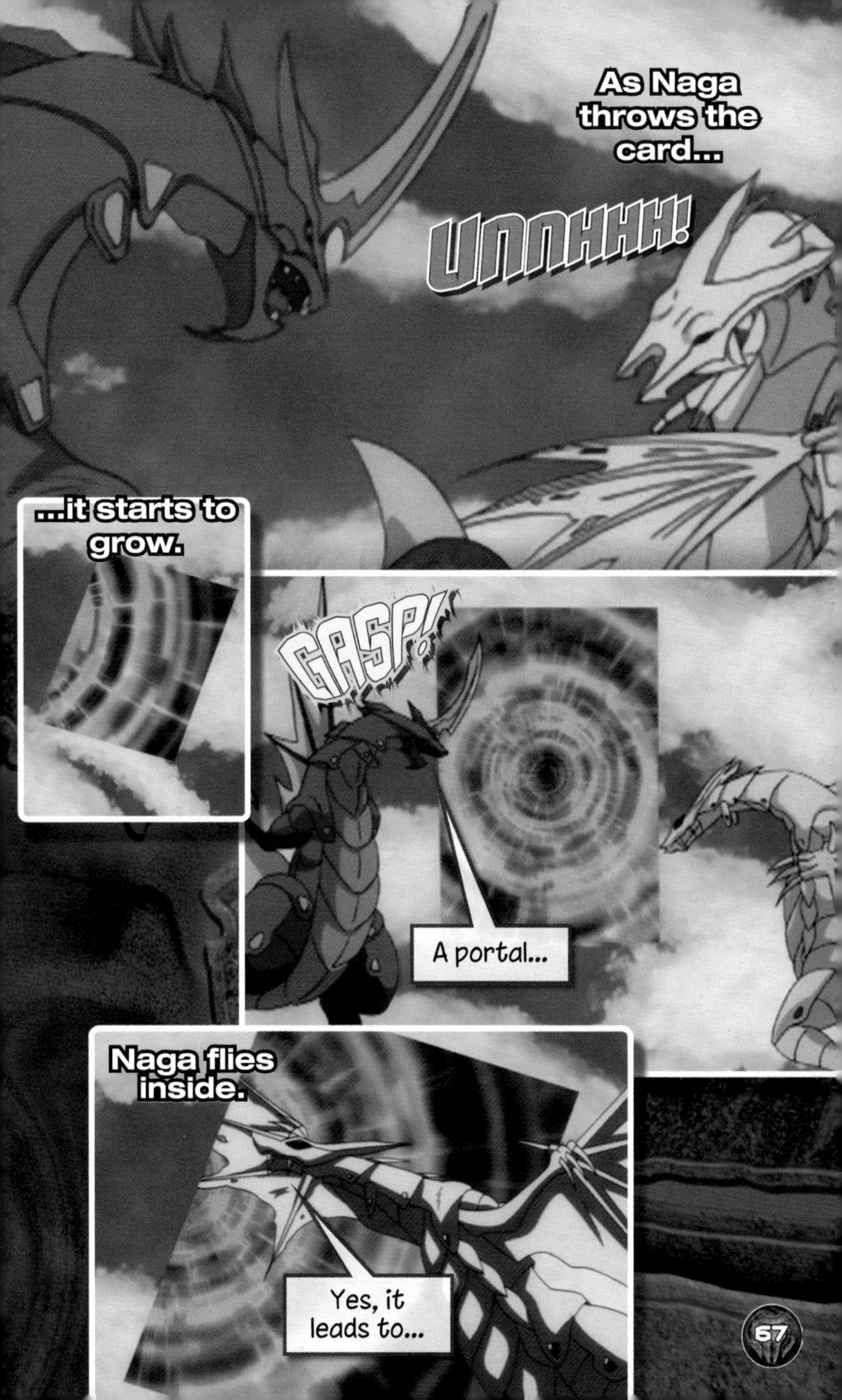
As Naga throws the card...
UNNHHH!
...it starts to grow.
GASP!
A portal...
Naga flies inside.
Yes, it leads to...

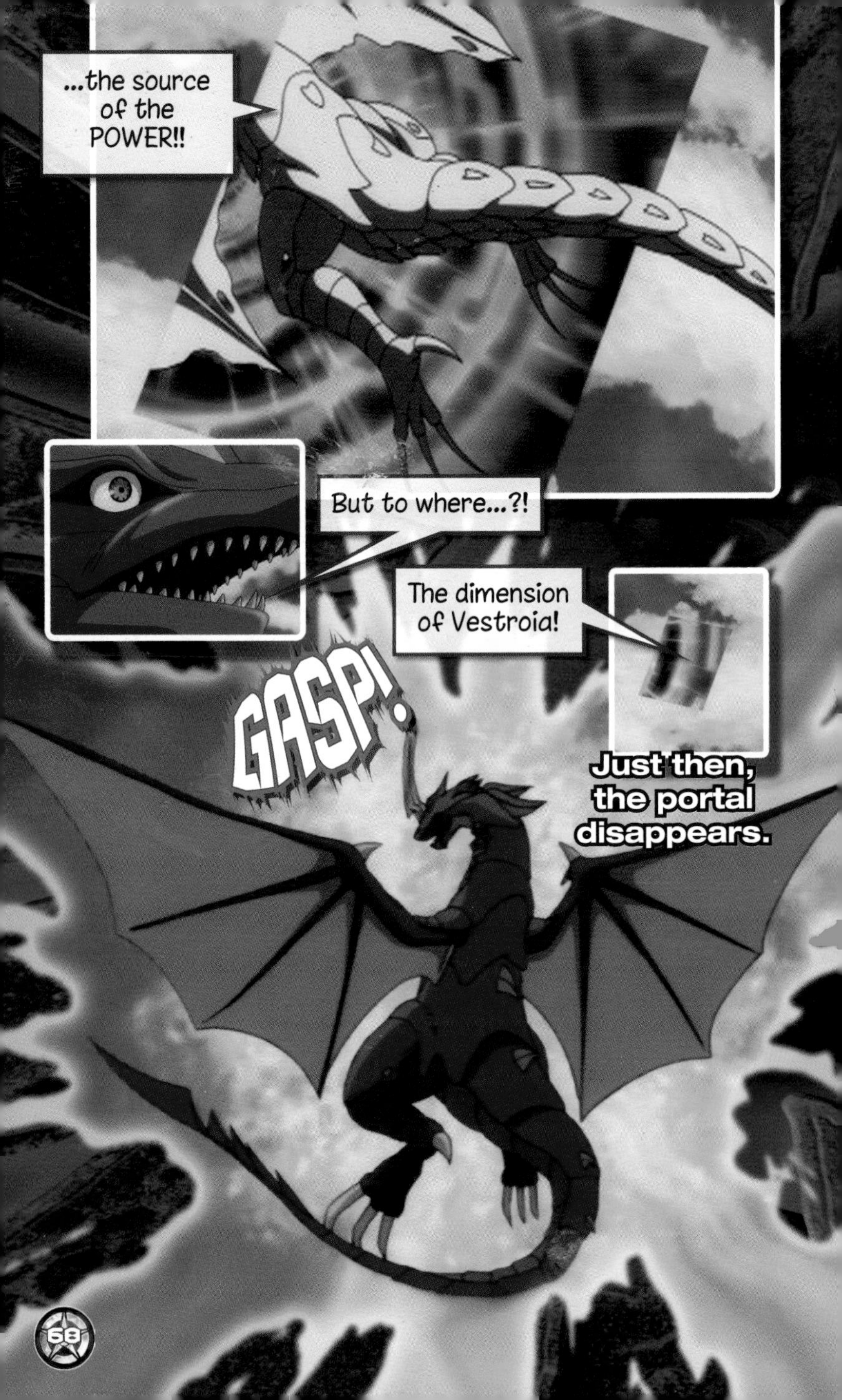
...the source of the POWER!!
But to where...?!
The dimension of Vestroia!
GASP!
Just then, the portal disappears.

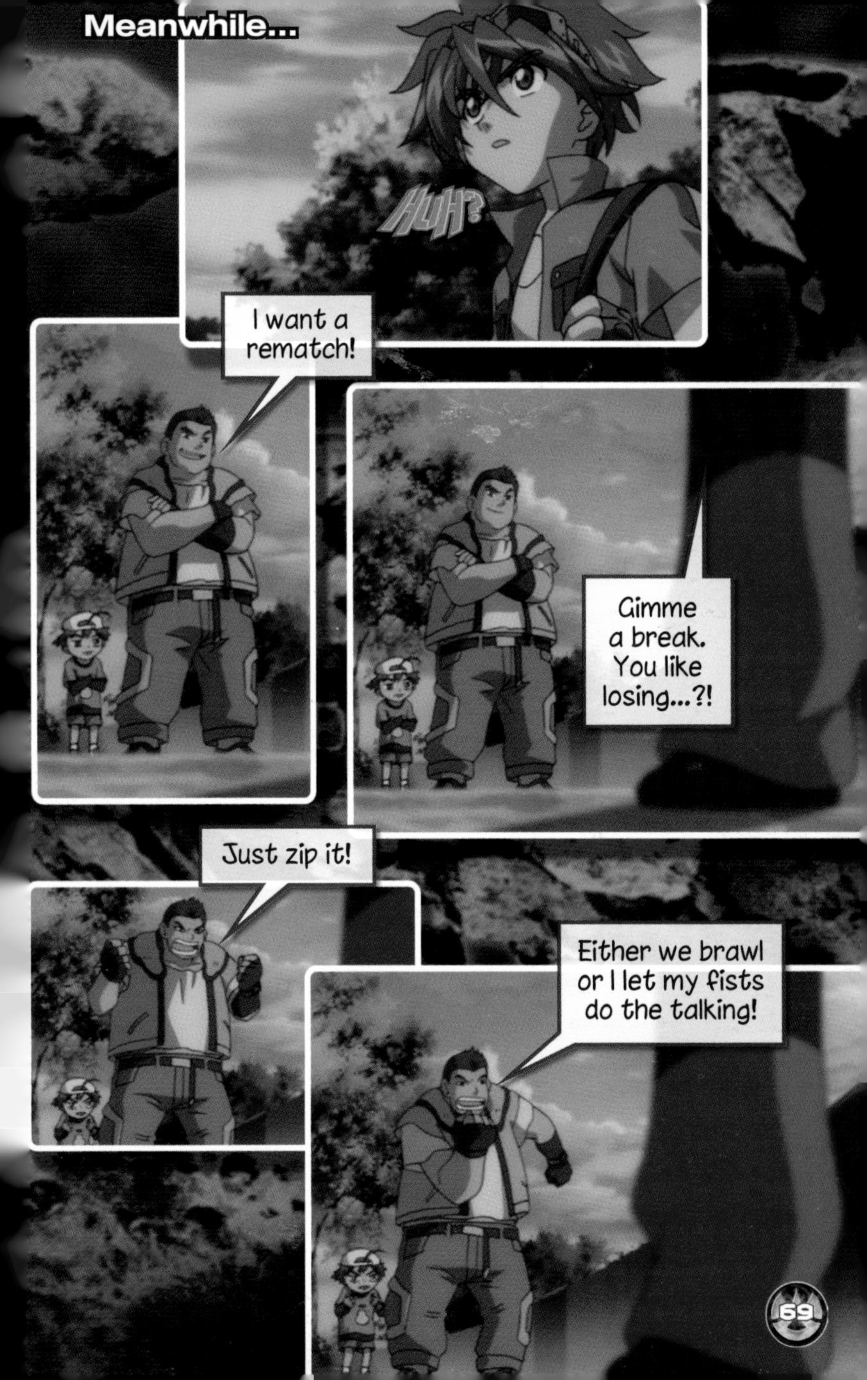
Meanwhile...
HUH?
I want a rematch!
Gimme a break. You like losing...?!
Just zip it!
Either we brawl or I let my fists do the talking!

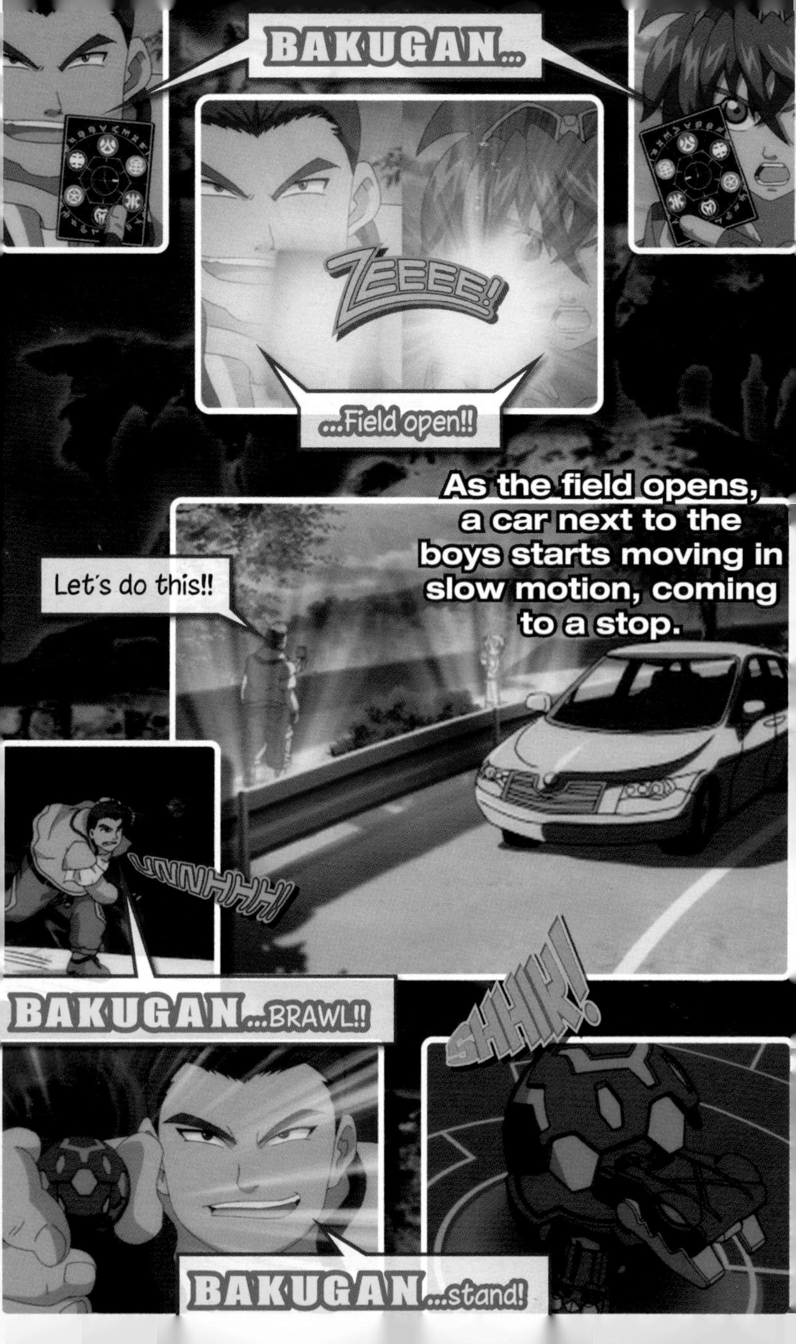
BAKUGAN...
ZEEEE!
...Field open!!
As the field opens, a car next to the boys starts moving in slow motion, coming to a stop.
Let's do this!!
UNNHHH!
BAKUGAN...BRAWL!!
SHHK!
BAKUGAN...stand!

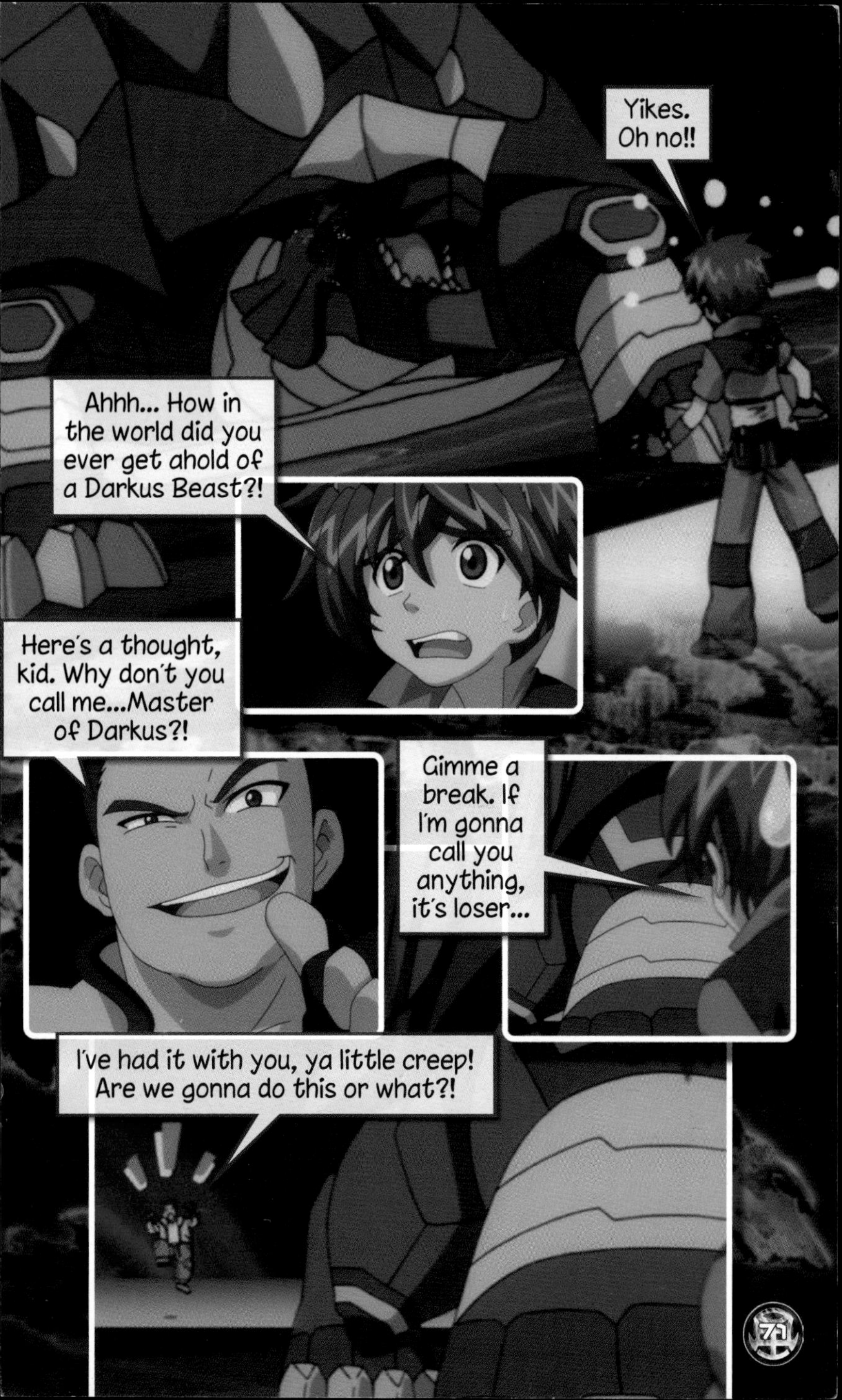

Yikes. Oh no!!
Ahhh... How in the world did you ever get ahold of a Darkus Beast?!
Here's a thought, kid. Why don't you call me...Master of Darkus?!
Gimme a break. If I'm gonna call you anything, it's loser...
I've had it with you, ya little creep! Are we gonna do this or what?!

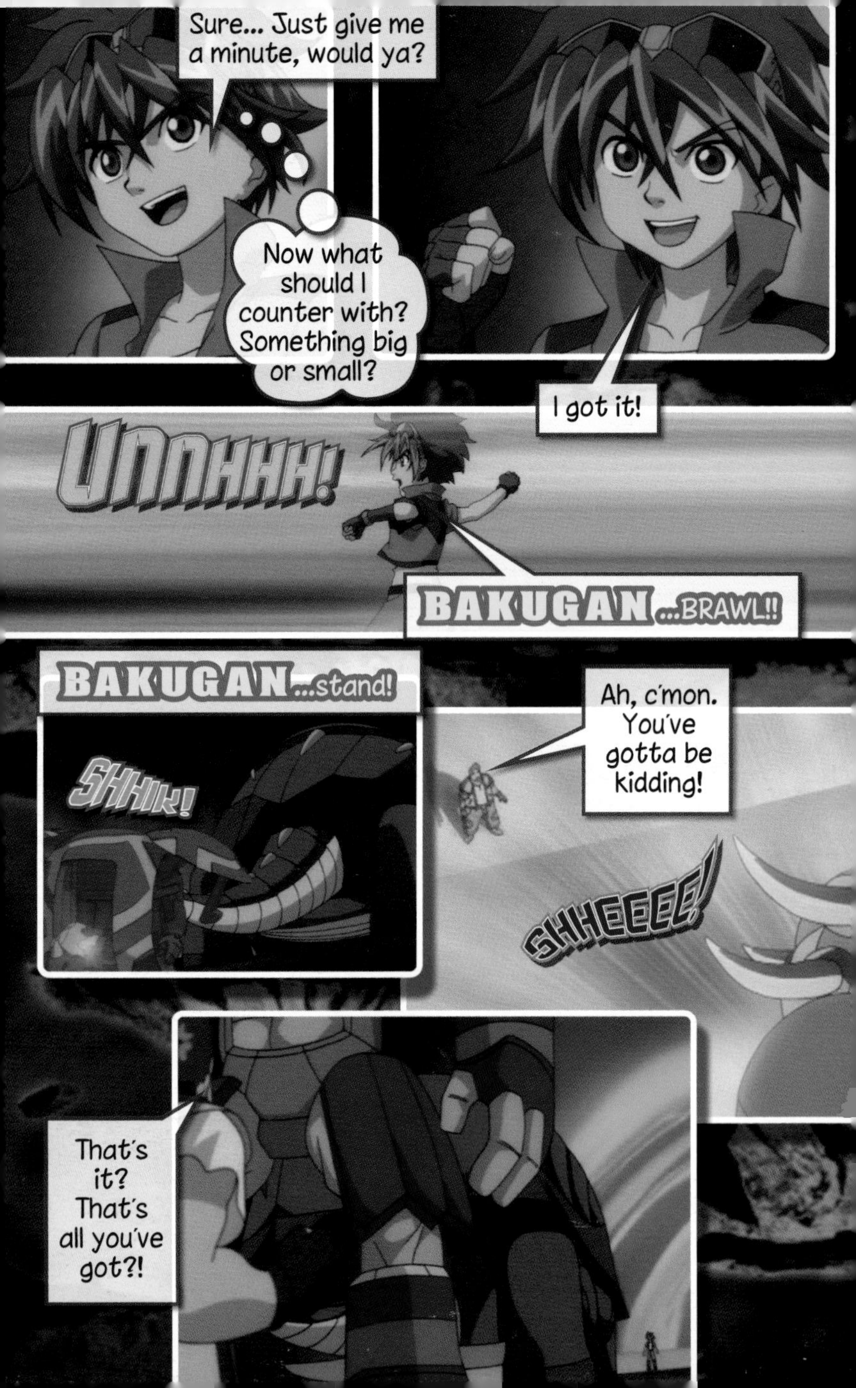
Sure... Just give me a minute, would ya?
Now what should I counter with? Something big or small?
I got it!
UNNHHH!
BAKUGAN ...BRAWL!!
BAKUGAN ...stand!
SHHIK!
Ah, c'mon. You've gotta be kidding!
SHHEEEE!
That's it? That's all you've got?!

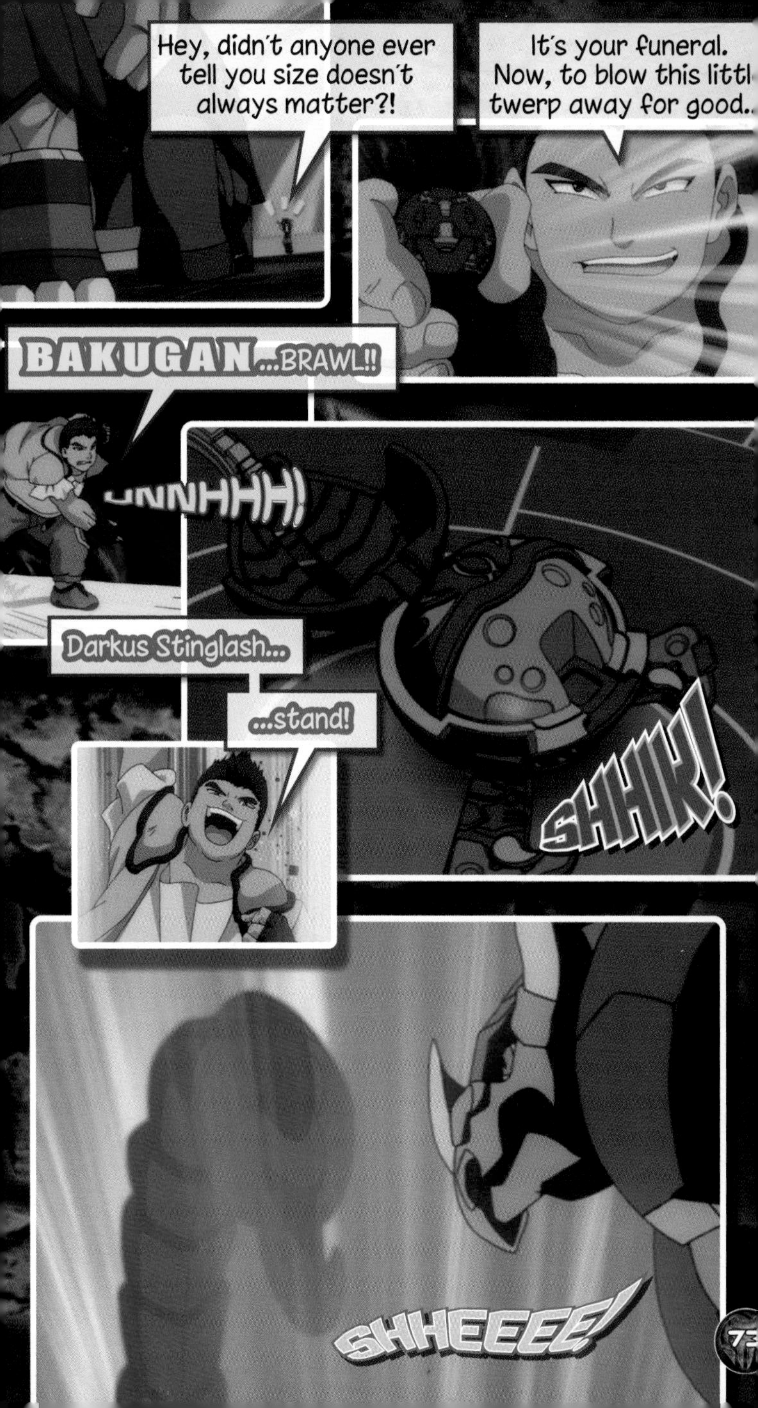

Hey, didn't anyone ever tell you size doesn't always matter?!
It's your funeral. Now, to blow this littl twerp away for good..
BAKUGAN...BRAWL!!
UNNHHH!
Darkus Stinglash...
...stand!
SHHIK!
SHHEEEE!

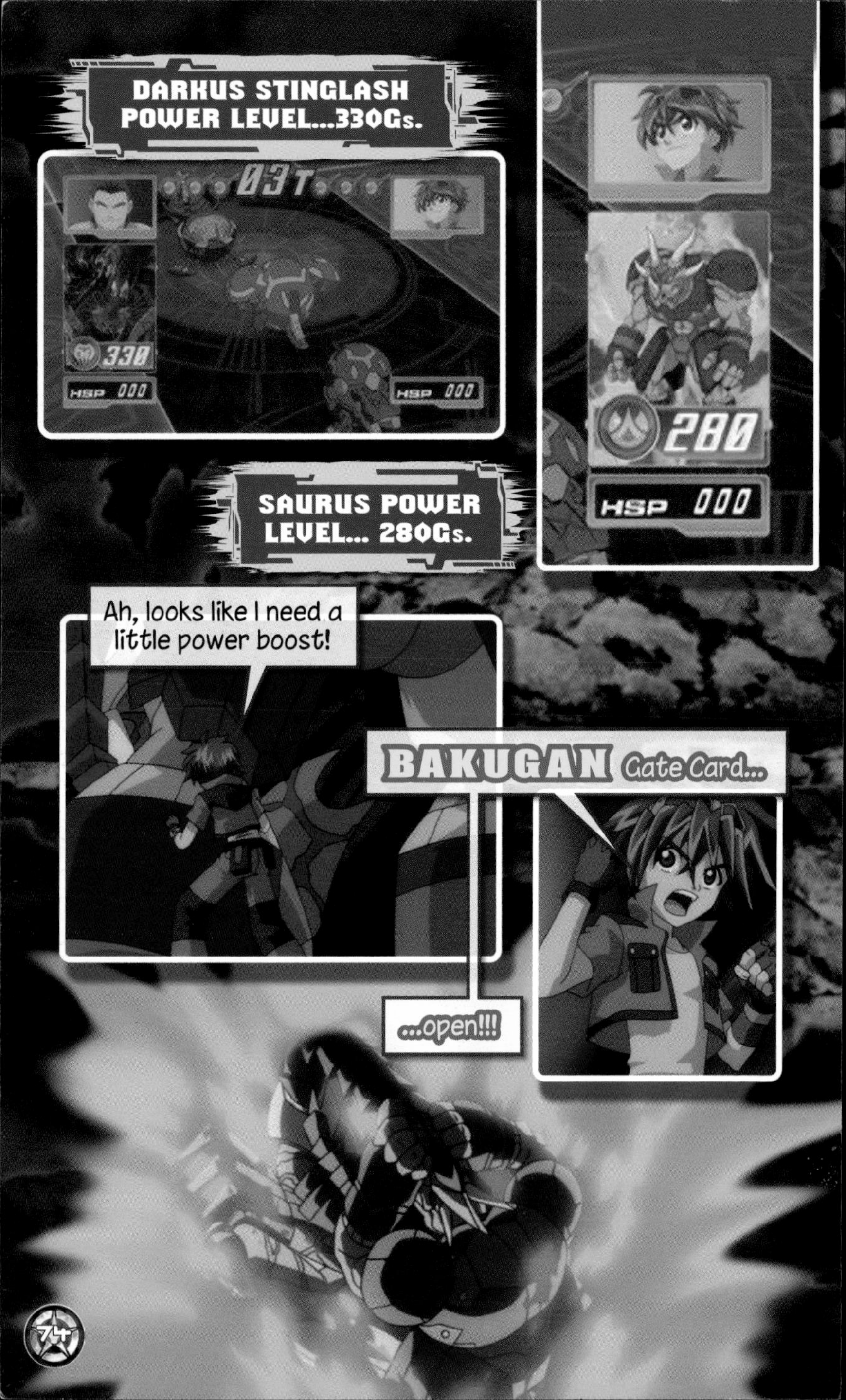

DARKUS STINGLASH POWER LEVEL...330Gs.
03T
330
HSP 000
HSP 000
280
HSP 000
SAURUS POWER LEVEL... 280Gs.
Ah, looks like I need a little power boost!
BAKUGAN Gate Card...
...open!!!

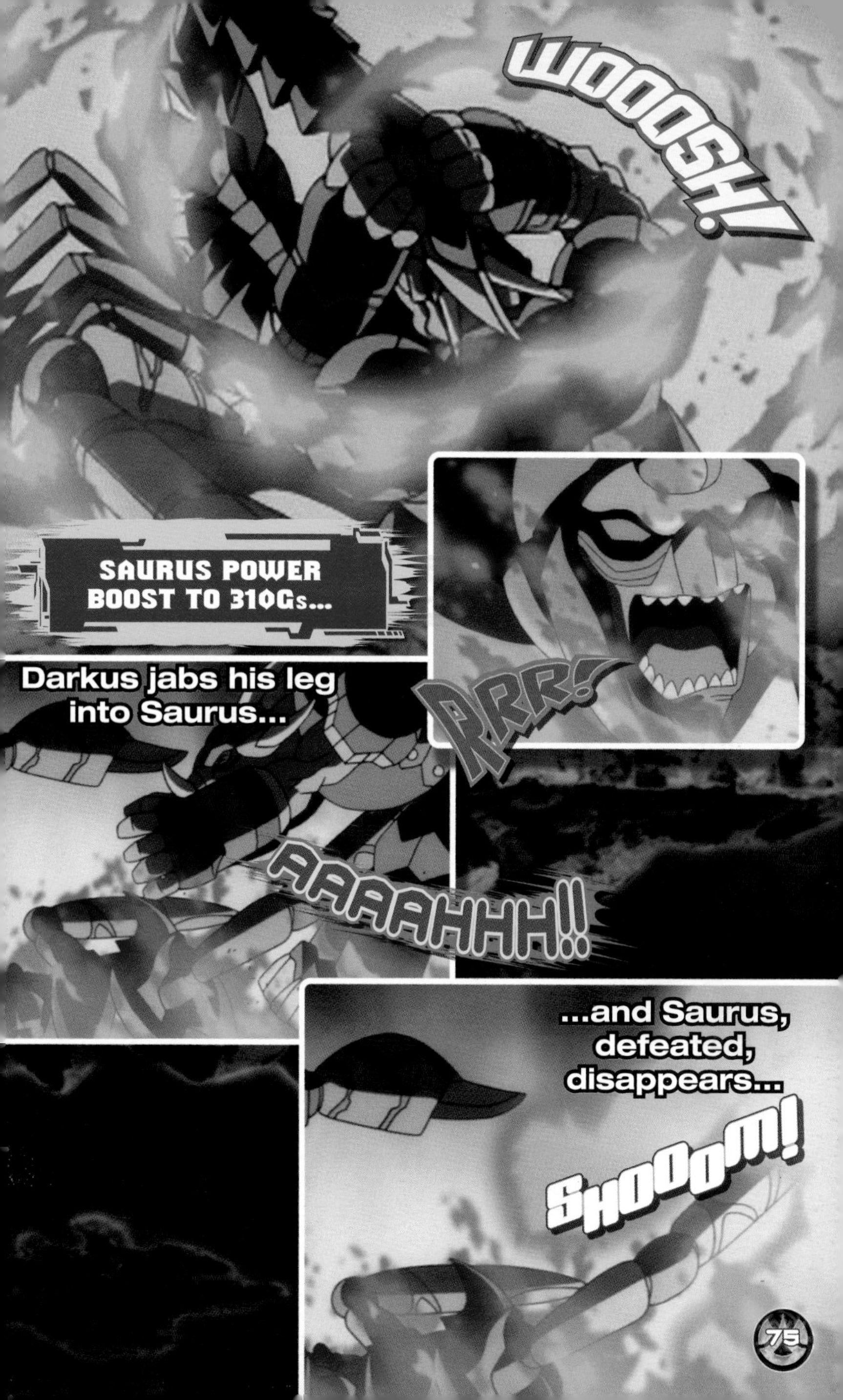
WOOOSH!
SAURUS POWER BOOST TO 310Gs...
RRR!
Darkus jabs his leg into Saurus...
AAAAHHH!!
...and Saurus, defeated, disappears...
SHOOOOM!

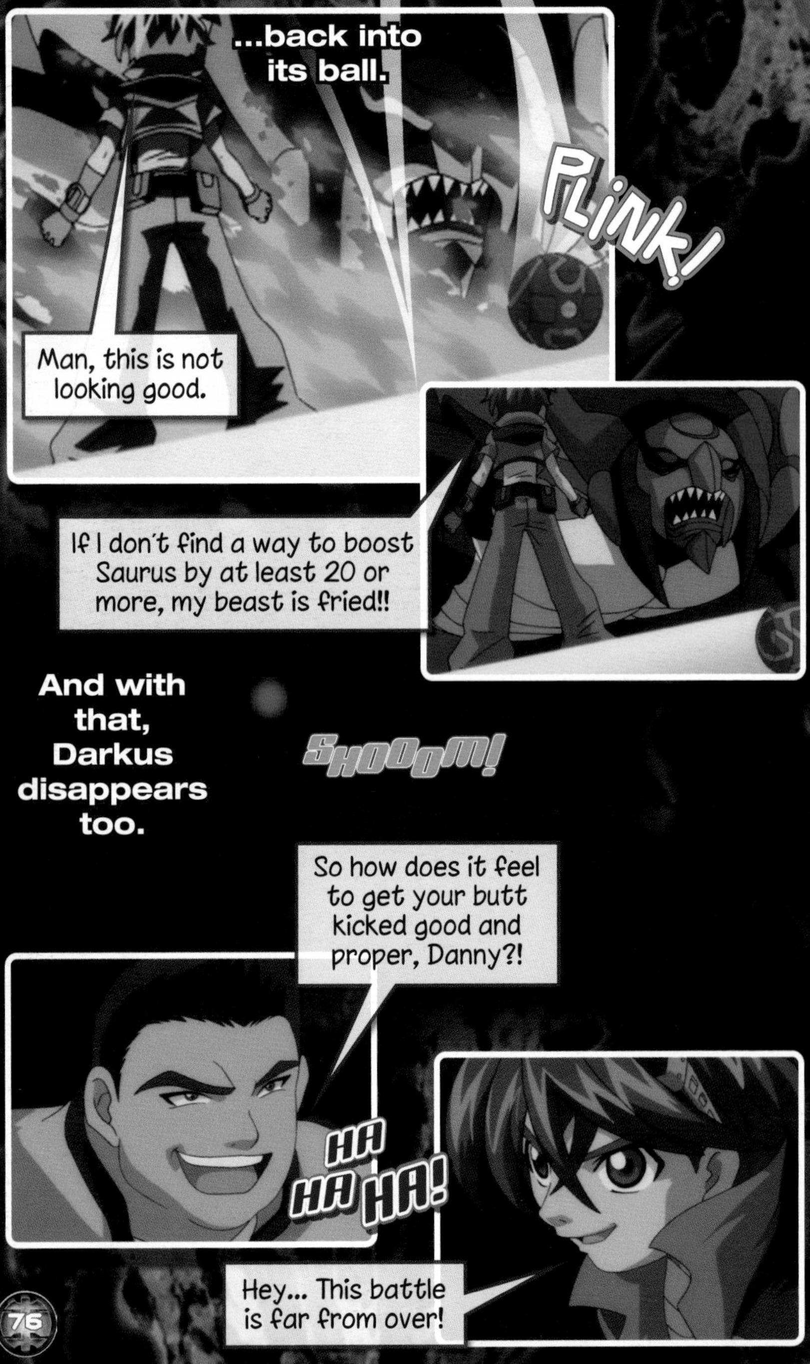
...back into its ball.
PLINK!
Man, this is not looking good.
If I don't find a way to boost Saurus by at least 20 or more, my beast is fried!!
And with that, Darkus disappears too.
SHOOOOM!
So how does it feel to get your butt kicked good and proper, Danny?!
HA HA HA!
Hey... This battle is far from over!

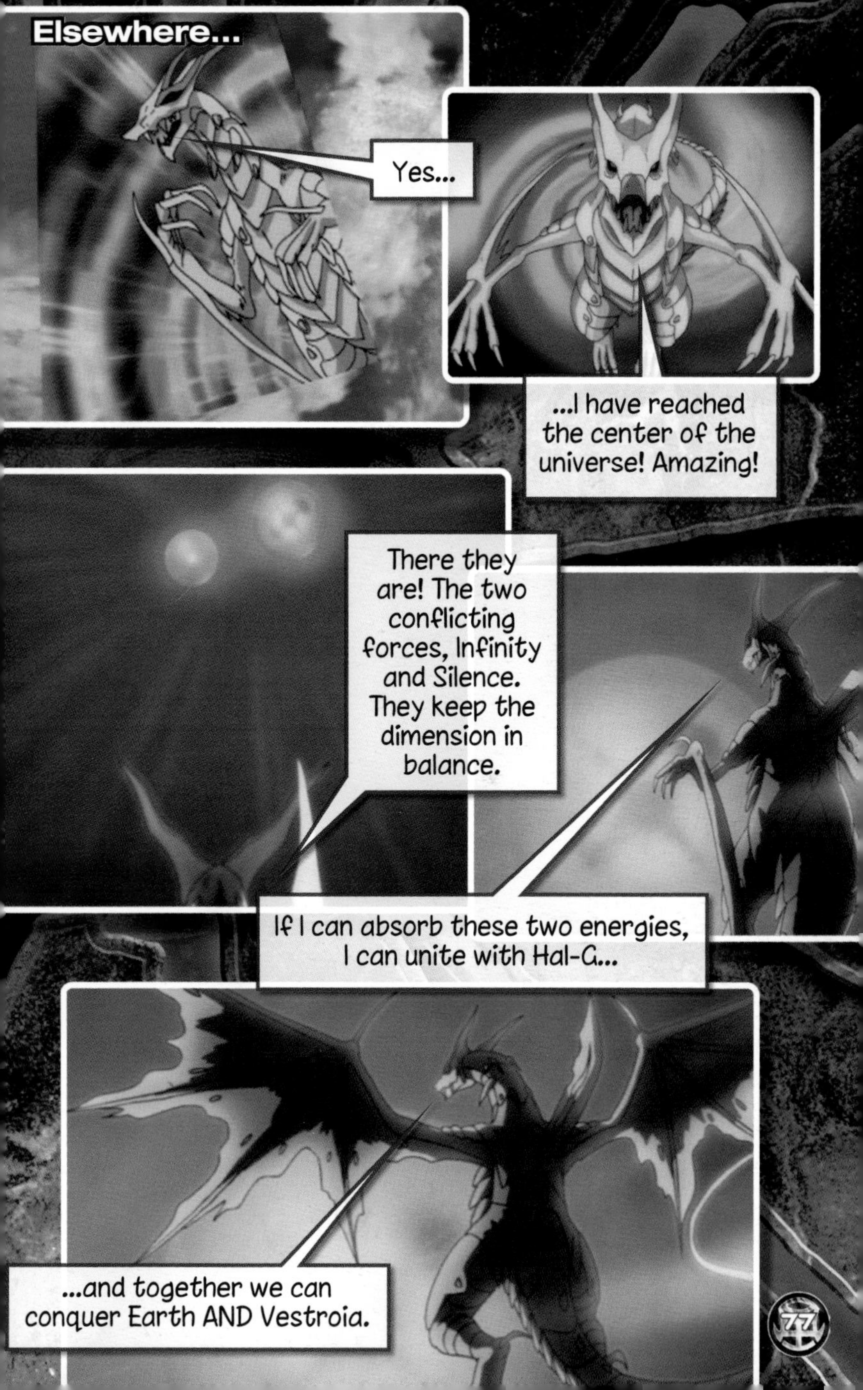

Elsewhere...
Yes...
...I have reached the center of the universe! Amazing!
There they are! The two conflicting forces, Infinity and Silence. They keep the dimension in balance.
If I can absorb these two energies, I can unite with Hal-G...
...and together we can conquer Earth AND Vestroia.

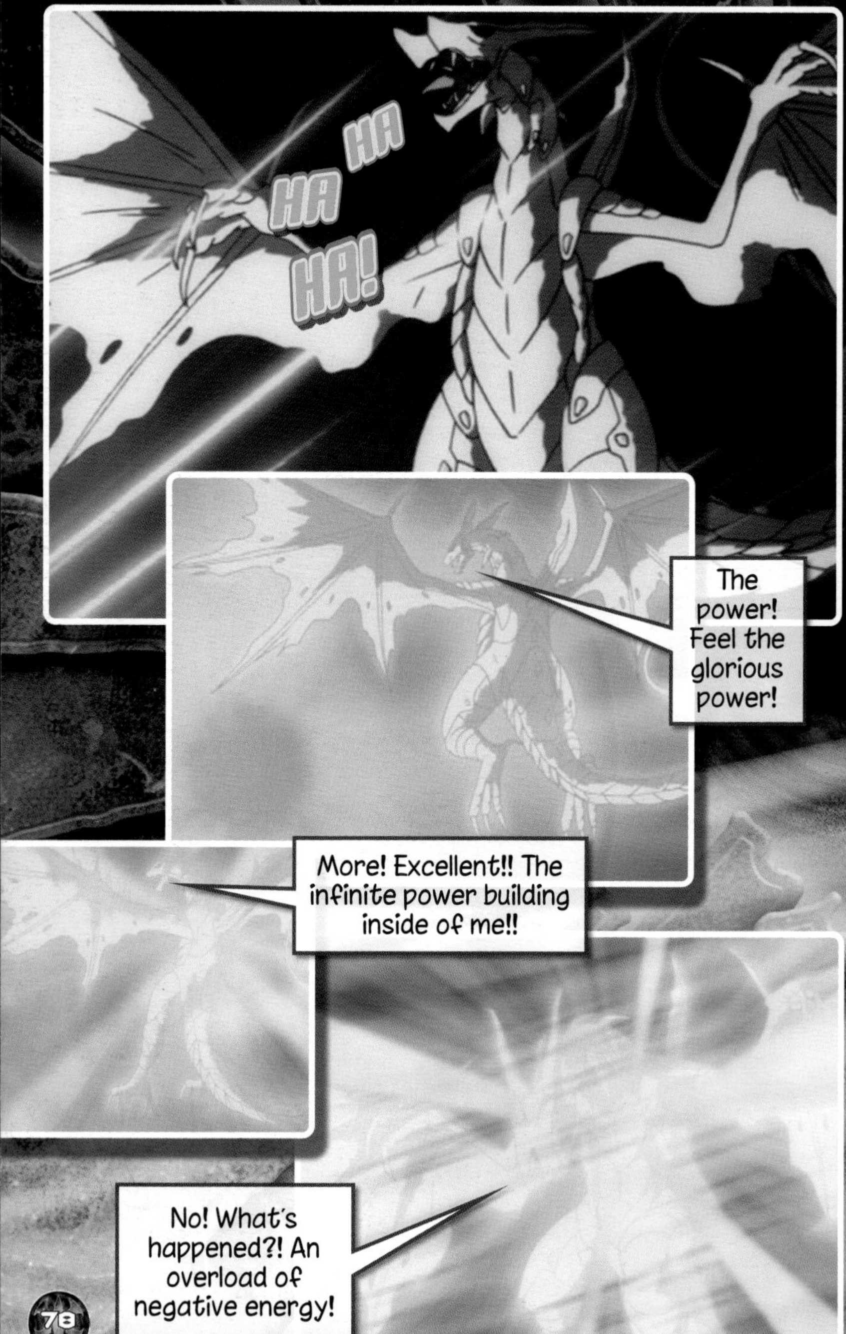

HA HA
HA!
The power! Feel the glorious power!
More! Excellent!! The infinite power building inside of me!!
No! What's happened?! An overload of negative energy!

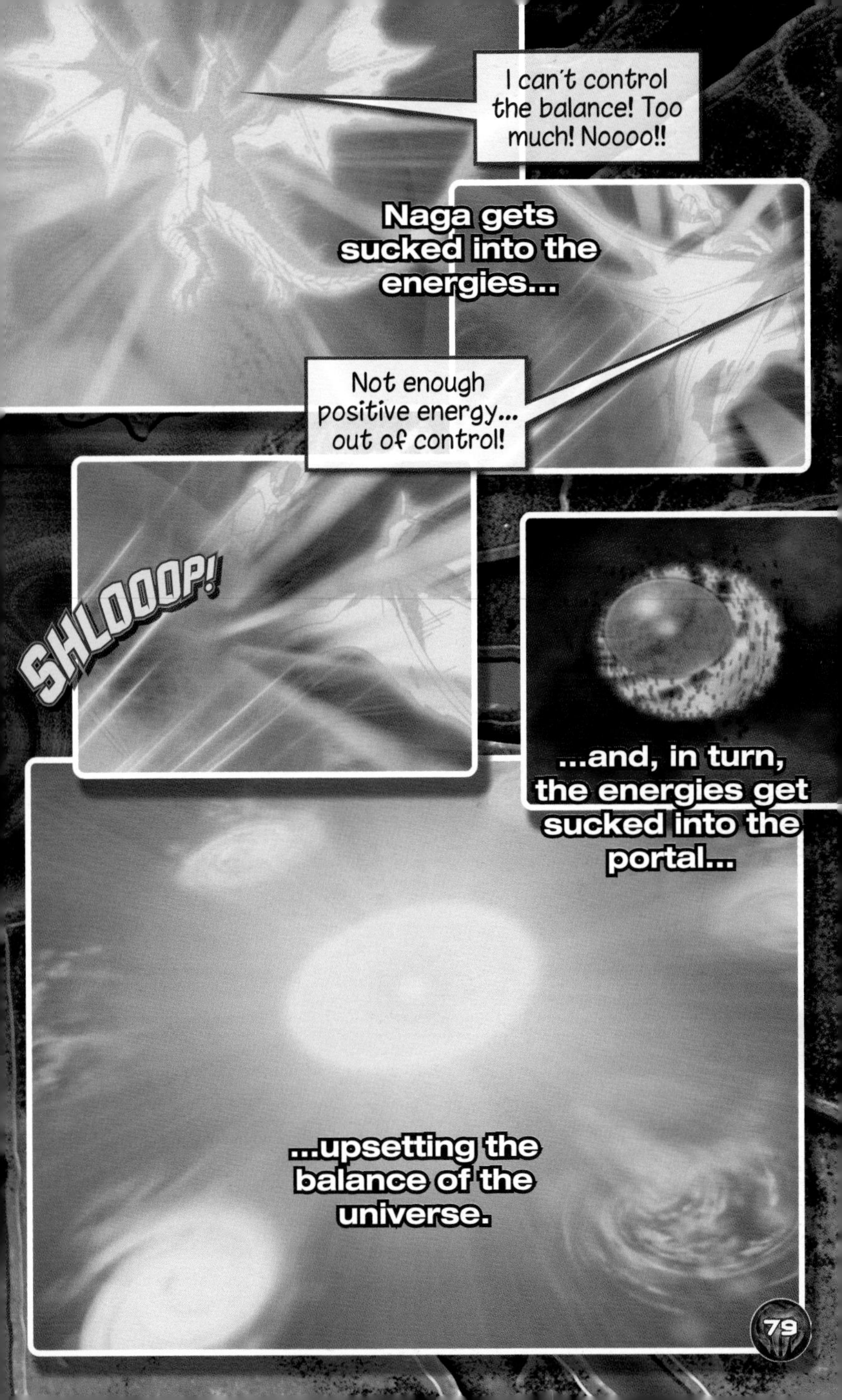

I can't control the balance! Too much! Noooo!!
Naga gets sucked into the energies...
Not enough positive energy... out of control!
SHLOOOP!
...and, in turn, the energies get sucked into the portal...
...upsetting the balance of the universe.

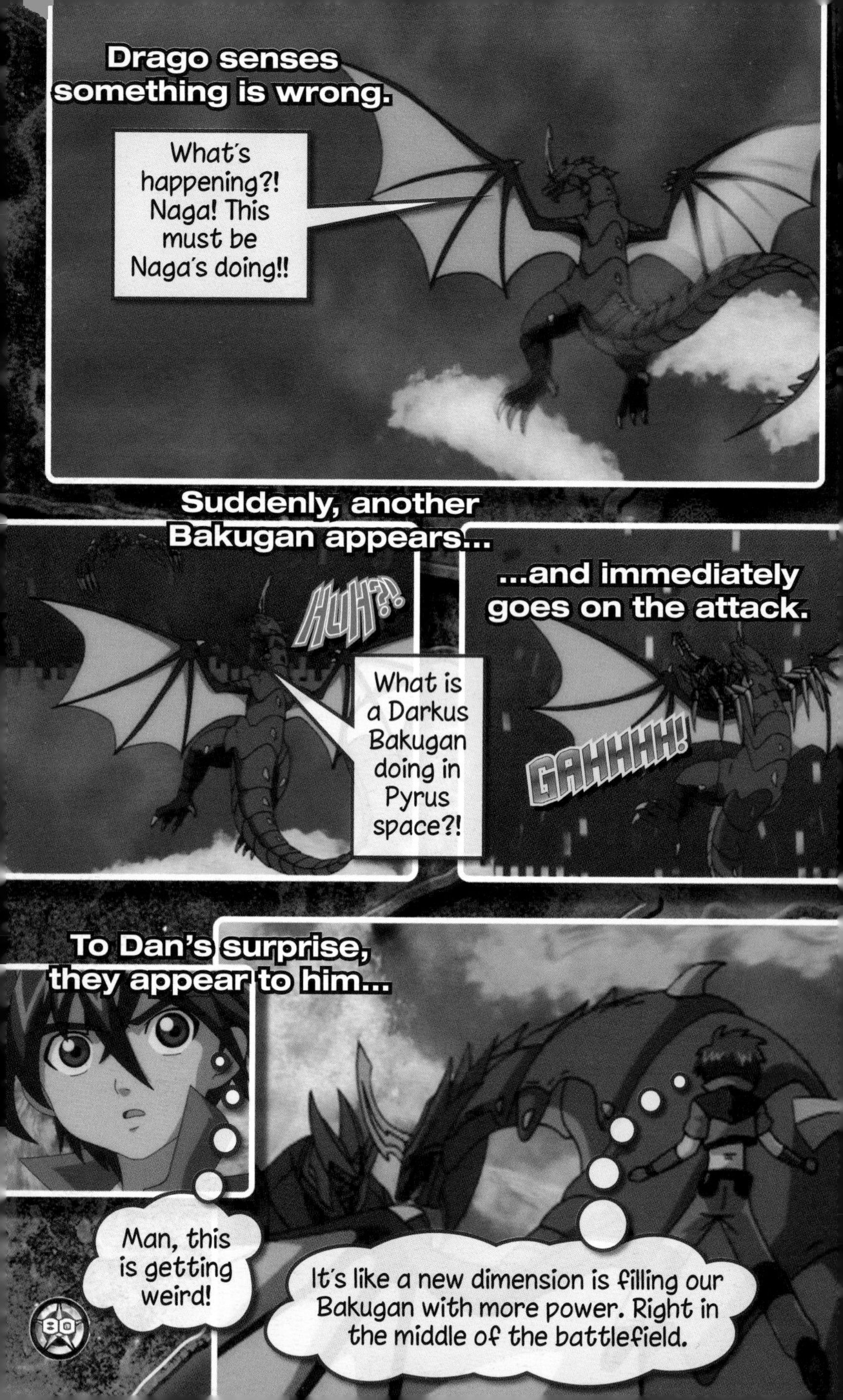
Drago senses something is wrong.
What's happening?! Naga! This must be Naga's doing!!
Suddenly, another Bakugan appears...
HUH?!
What is a Darkus Bakugan doing in Pyrus space?!
...and immediately goes on the attack.
GAHHHH!
To Dan's surprise, they appear to him...
Man, this is getting weird!
It's like a new dimension is filling our Bakugan with more power. Right in the middle of the battlefield.
80

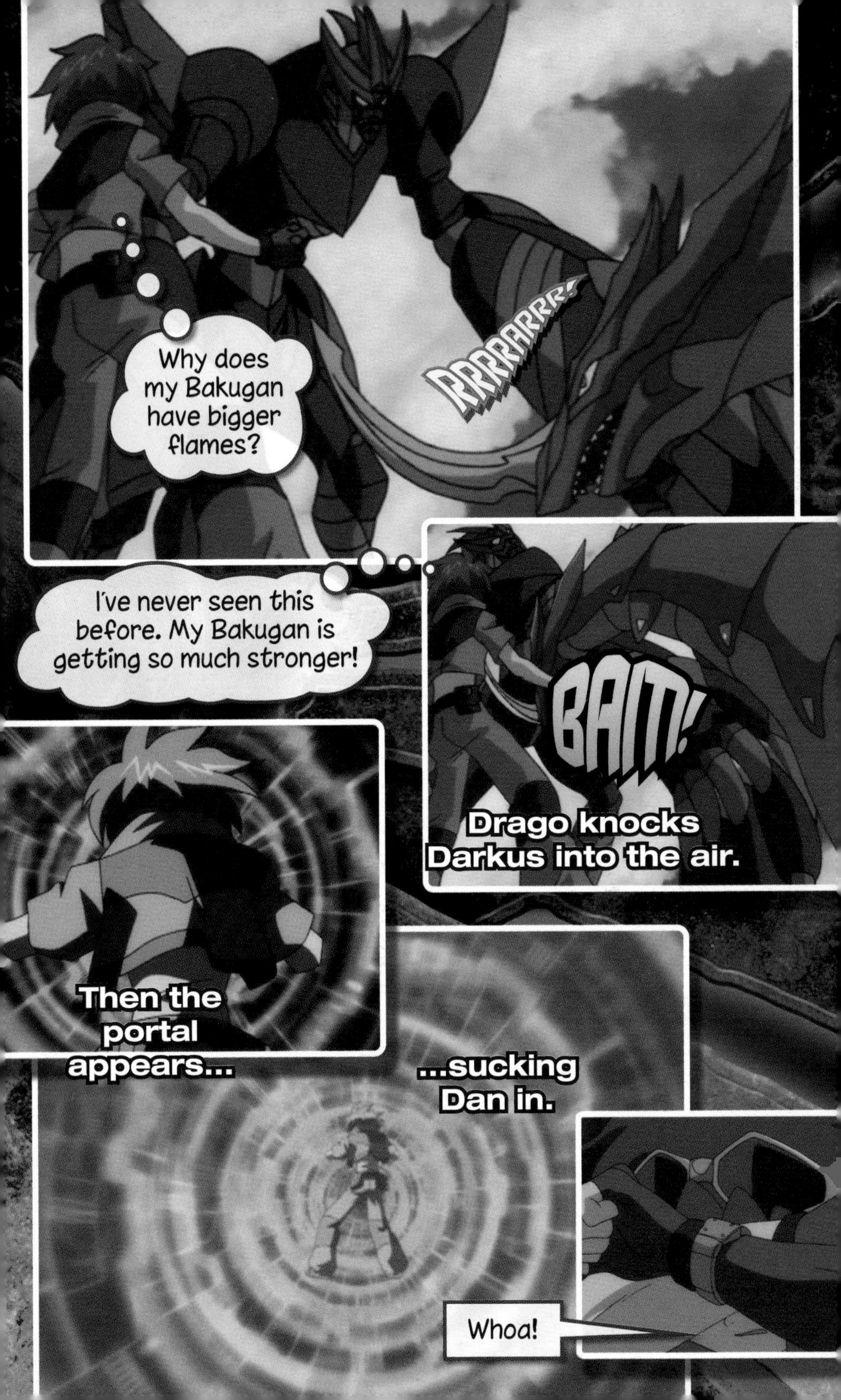
Why does my Bakugan have bigger flames?
RRRRARRR!
I've never seen this before. My Bakugan is getting so much stronger!
BAM!
Drago knocks Darkus into the air.
Then the portal appears...
...sucking Dan in.
Whoa!

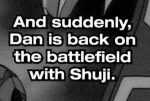

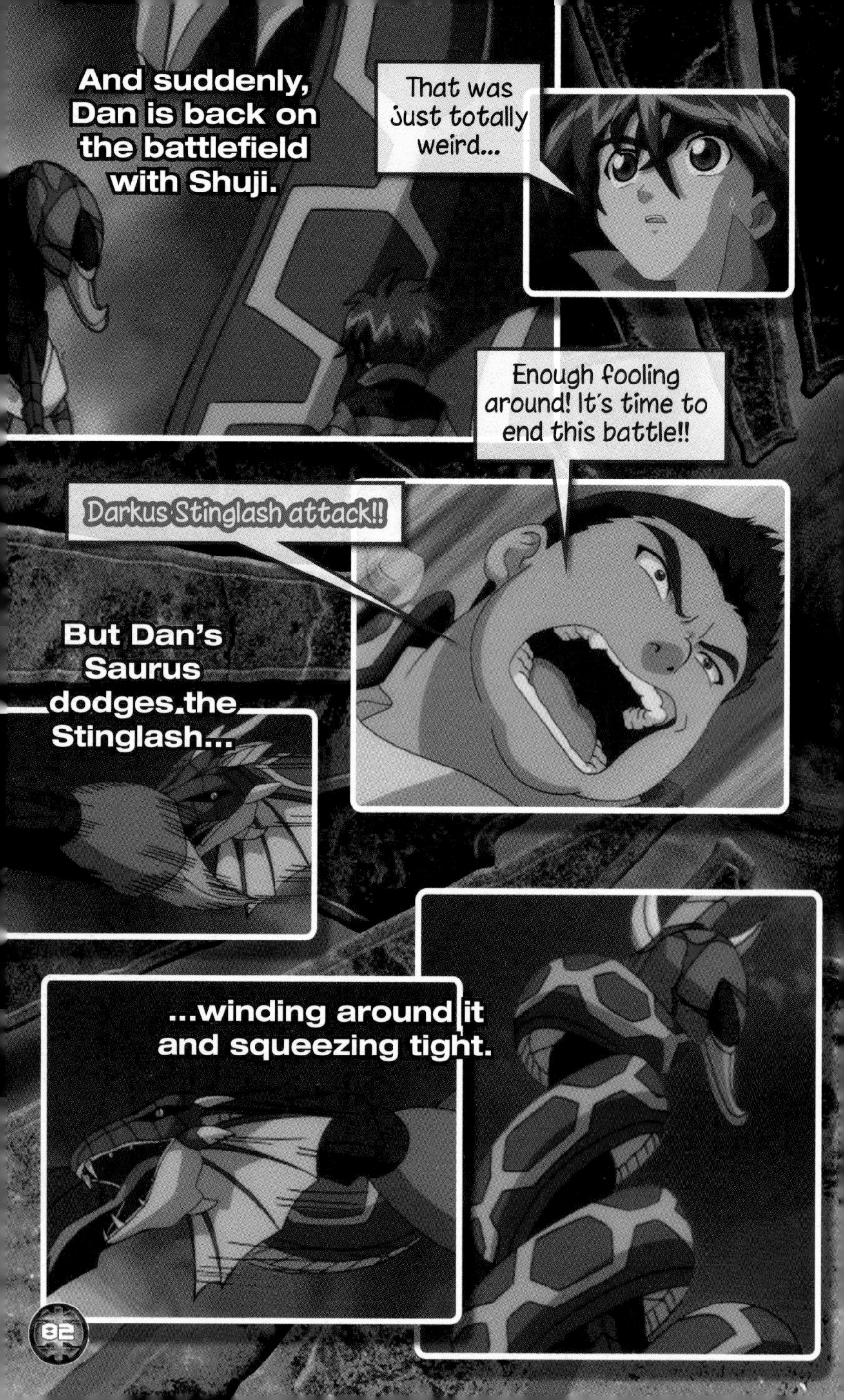

And suddenly, Dan is back on the battlefield with Shuji.

That was just totally weird...

Enough fooling around! It's time to end this battle!!

Darkus Stinglash attack!!

But Dan's Saurus dodges the Stinglash...

...winding around it and squeezing tight.

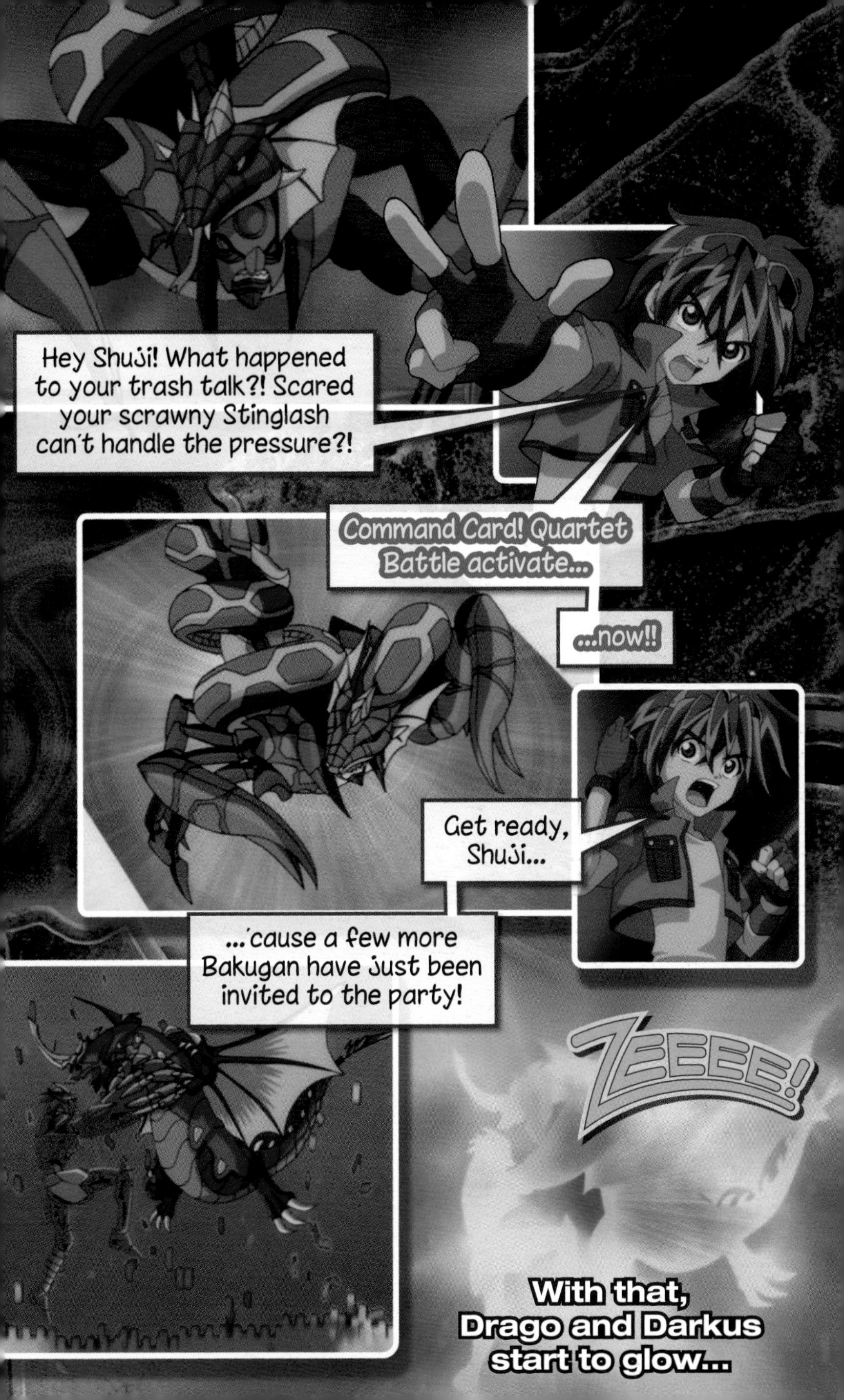

Hey Shuji! What happened to your trash talk?! Scared your scrawny Stinglash can't handle the pressure?!
Command Card! Quartet Battle activate...
...now!!
Get ready, Shuji...
...'cause a few more Bakugan have just been invited to the party!
ZEEEE!
With that, Drago and Darkus start to glow...

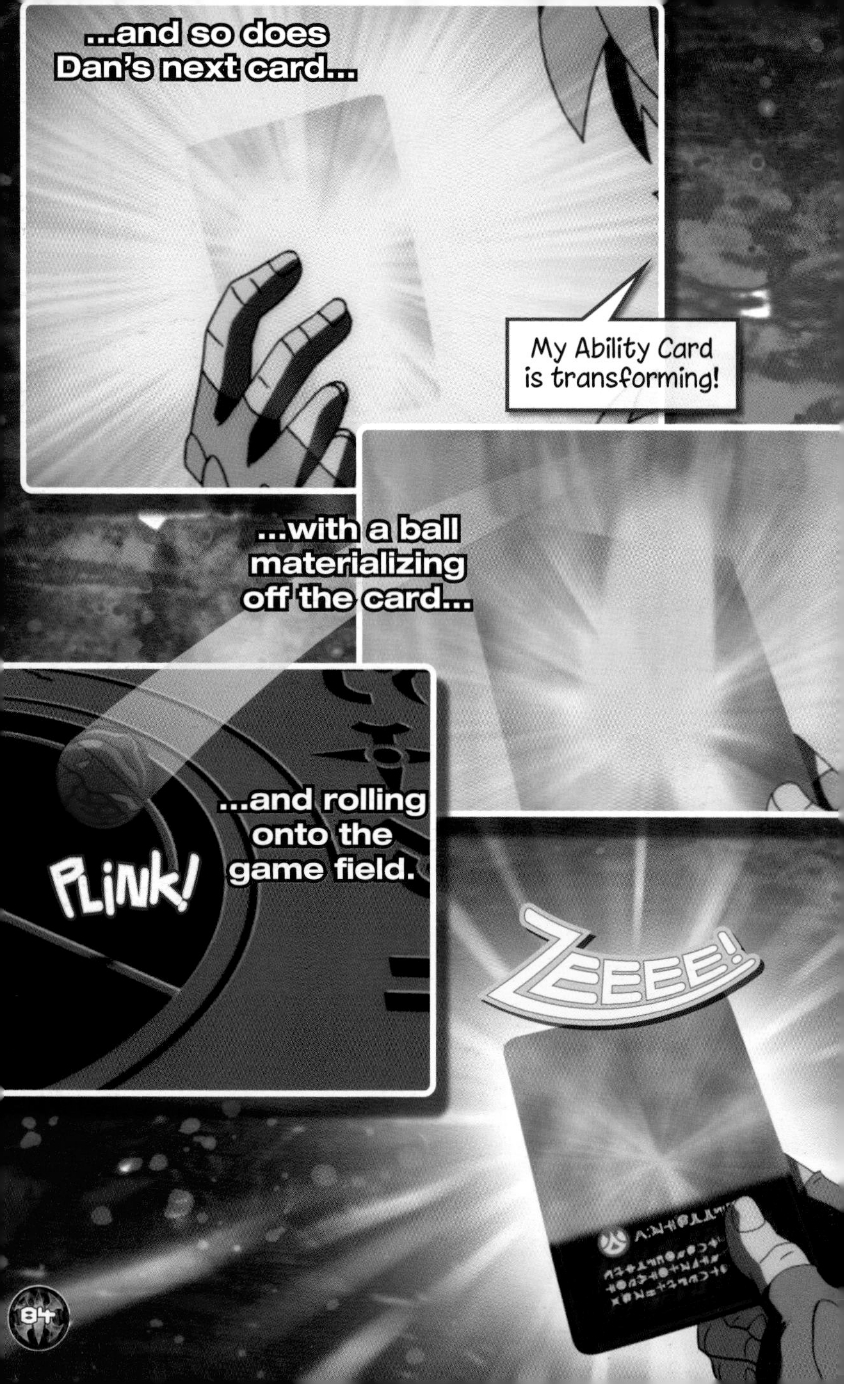
...and so does Dan's next card...
My Ability Card is transforming!
...with a ball materializing off the card...
...and rolling onto the game field.
PLINK!
ZEEEE!

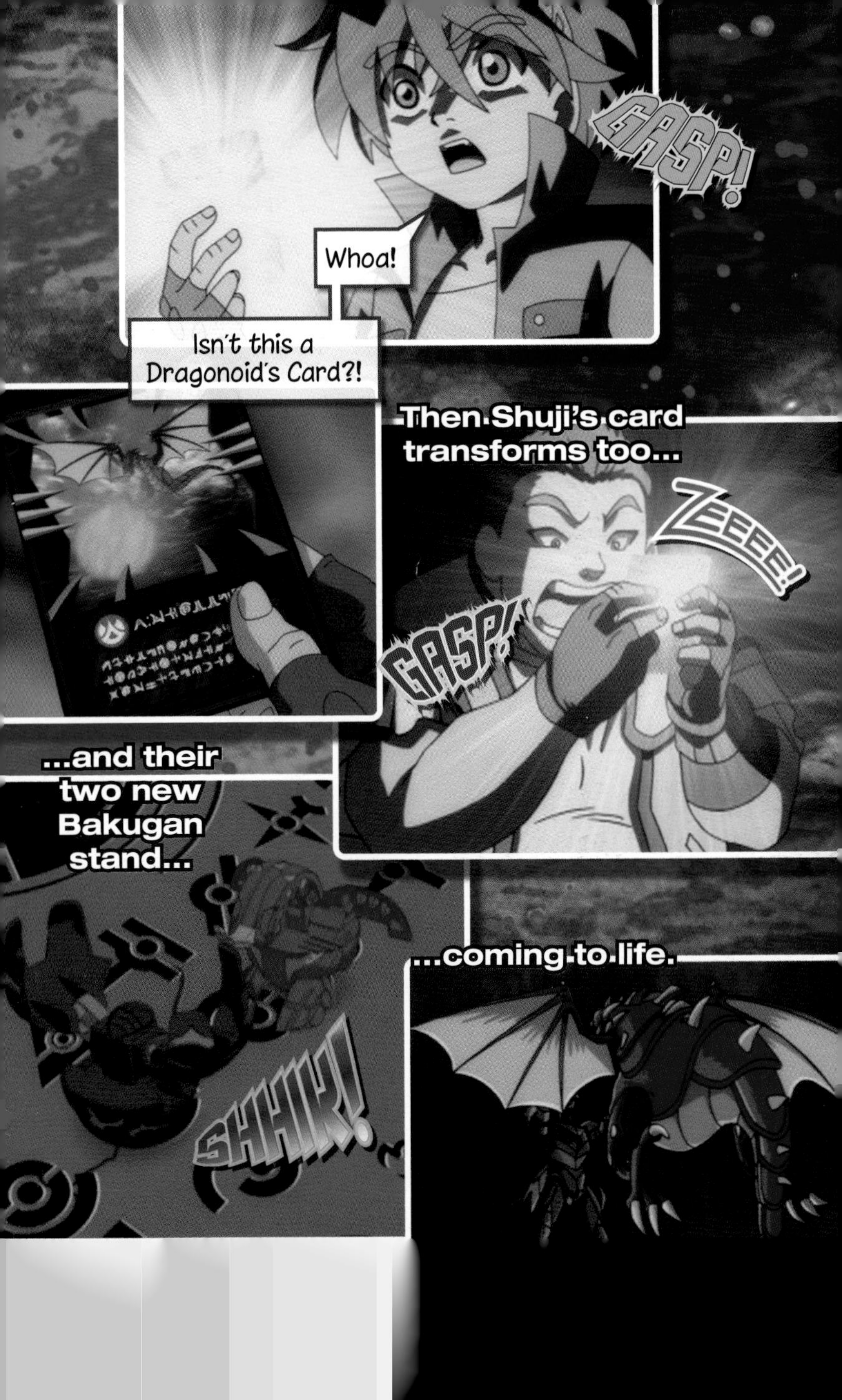
GASP!
Whoa!
Isn't this a Dragonoid's Card?!
Then Shuji's card transforms too...
ZEEEE!
GASP!
...and their two new Bakugan stand...
SHHIK!
...coming to life.

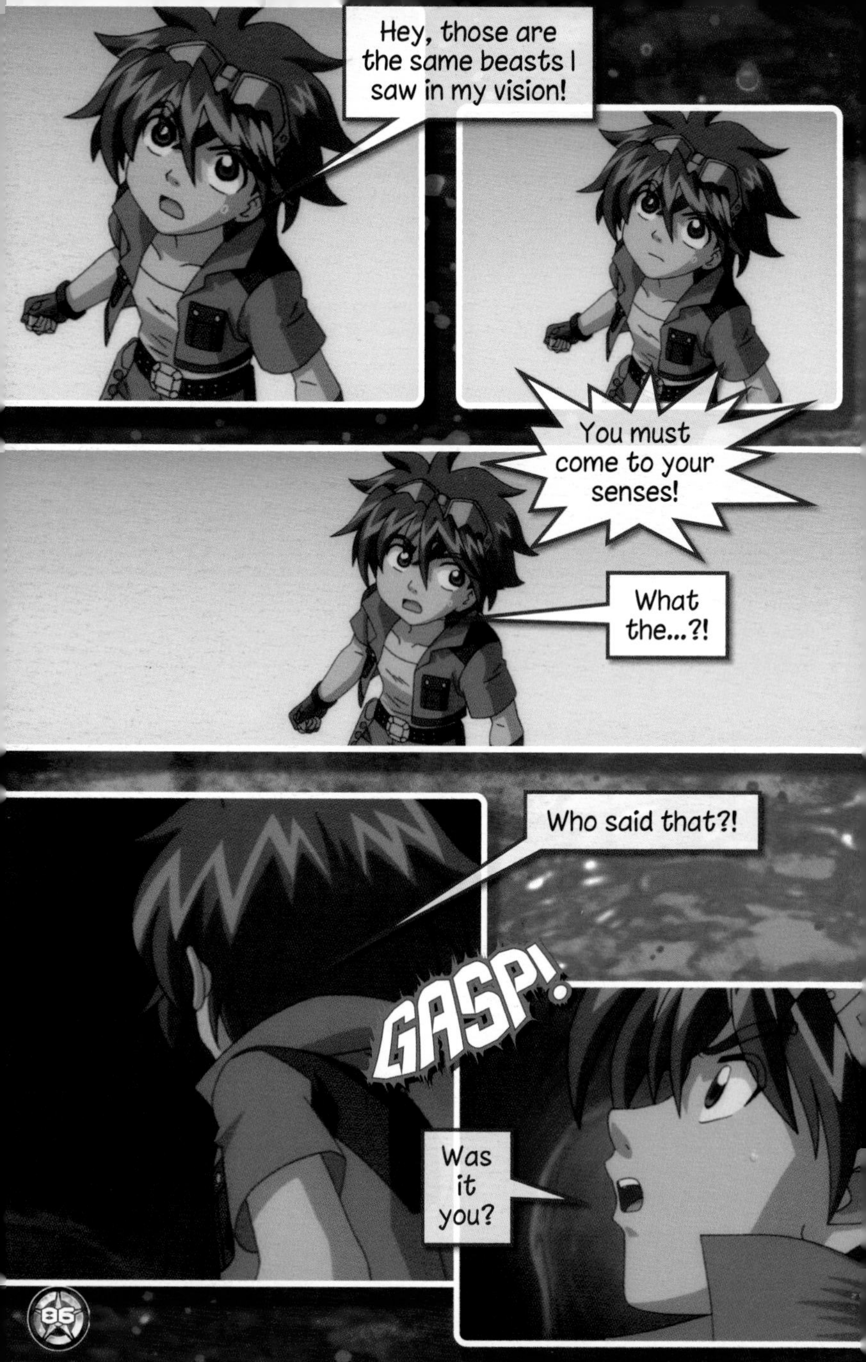
Hey, those are the same beasts I saw in my vision!
You must come to your senses!
What the...?!
Who said that?!
GASP!
Was it you?

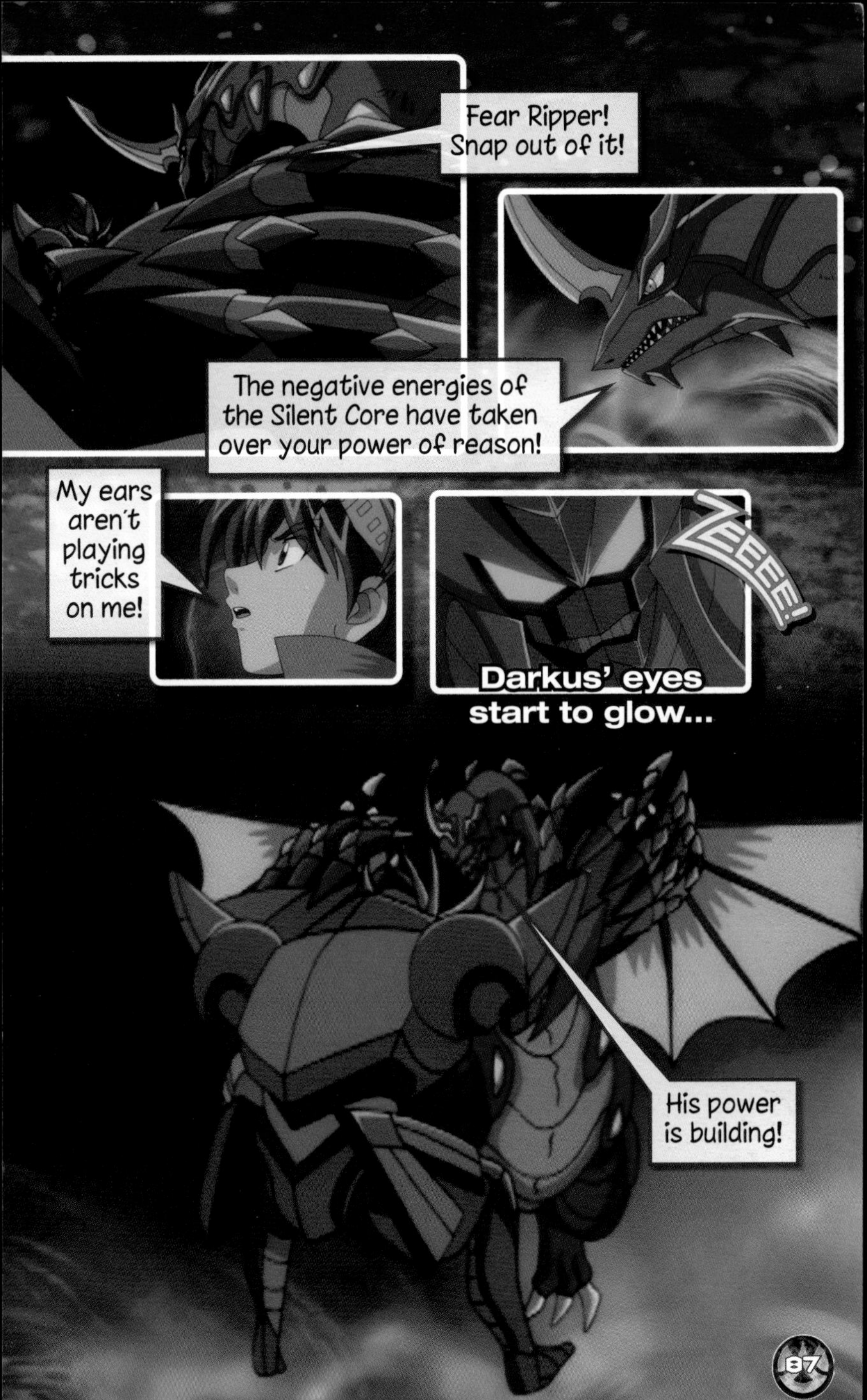
Fear Ripper!
Snap out of it!
The negative energies of the Silent Core have taken over your power of reason!
My ears aren't playing tricks on me!
ZEEEE!
Darkus' eyes start to glow...
His power is building!

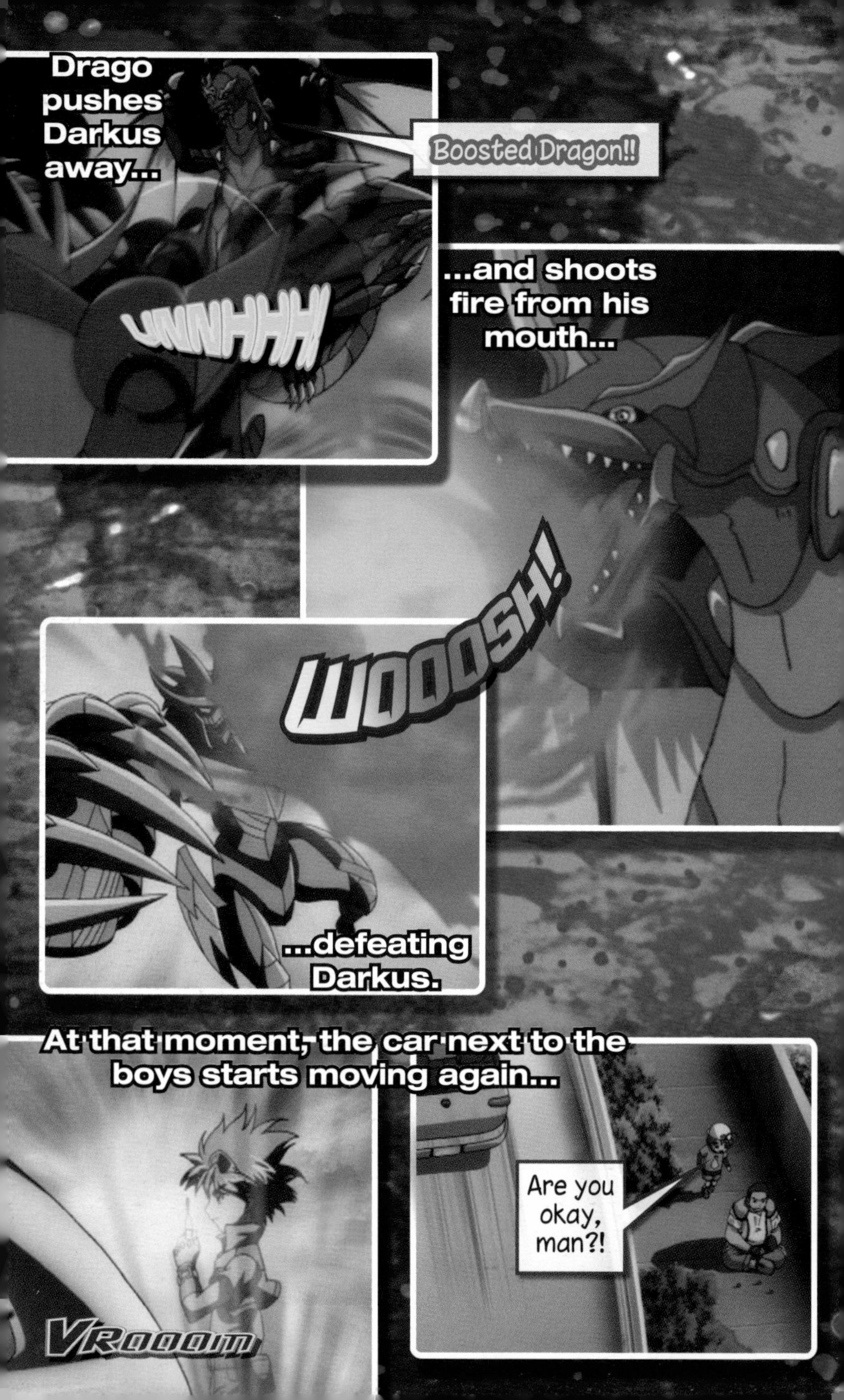
Drago pushes Darkus away...
Boosted Dragon!!
UNNHHH!
...and shoots fire from his mouth...
WOOOSH!
...defeating Darkus.
At that moment, the car next to the boys starts moving again...
VROOOM
Are you okay, man?!

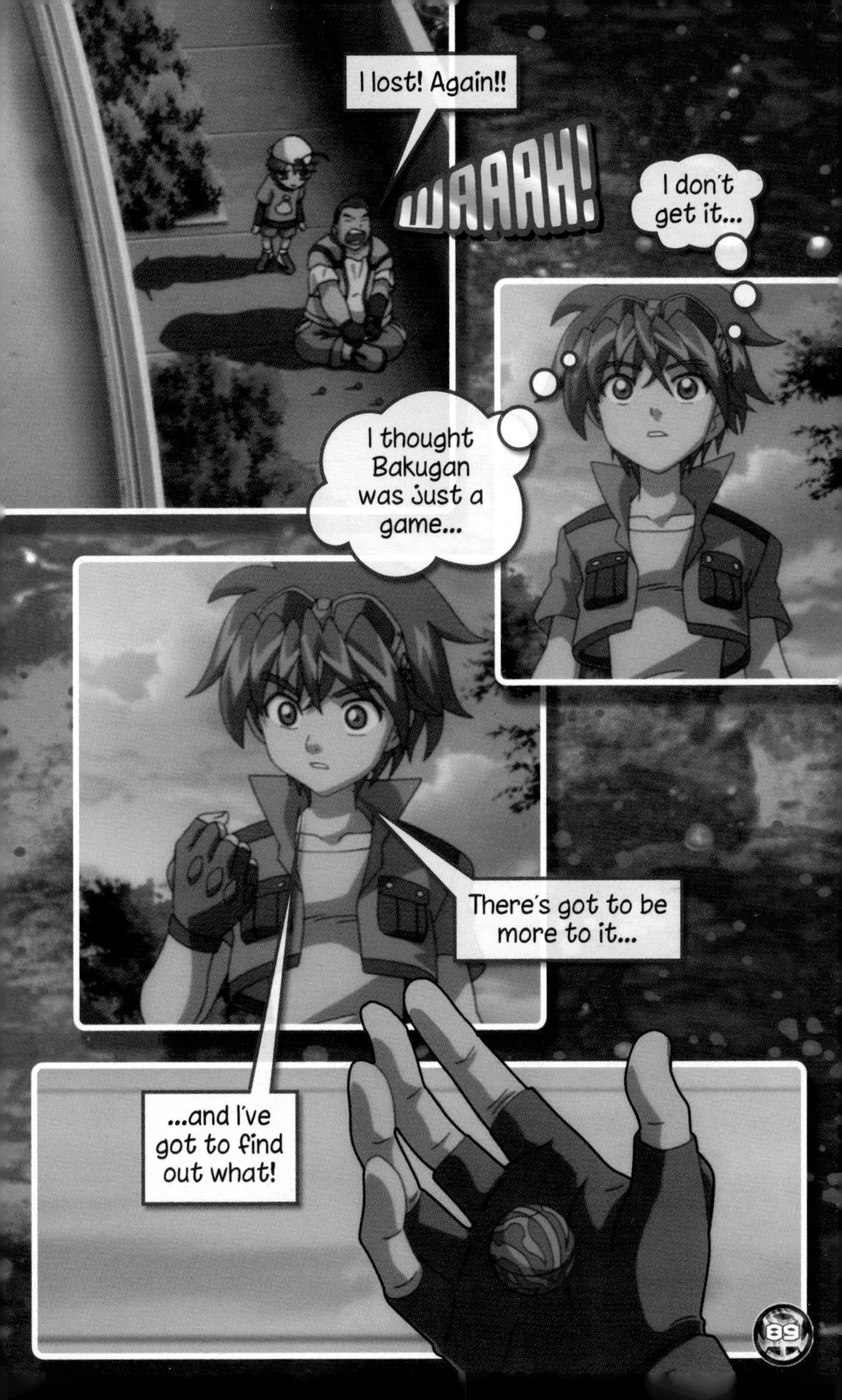

I lost! Again!!
WAAAH!
I don't get it...
I thought Bakugan was just a game...
There's got to be more to it...
...and I've got to find out what!

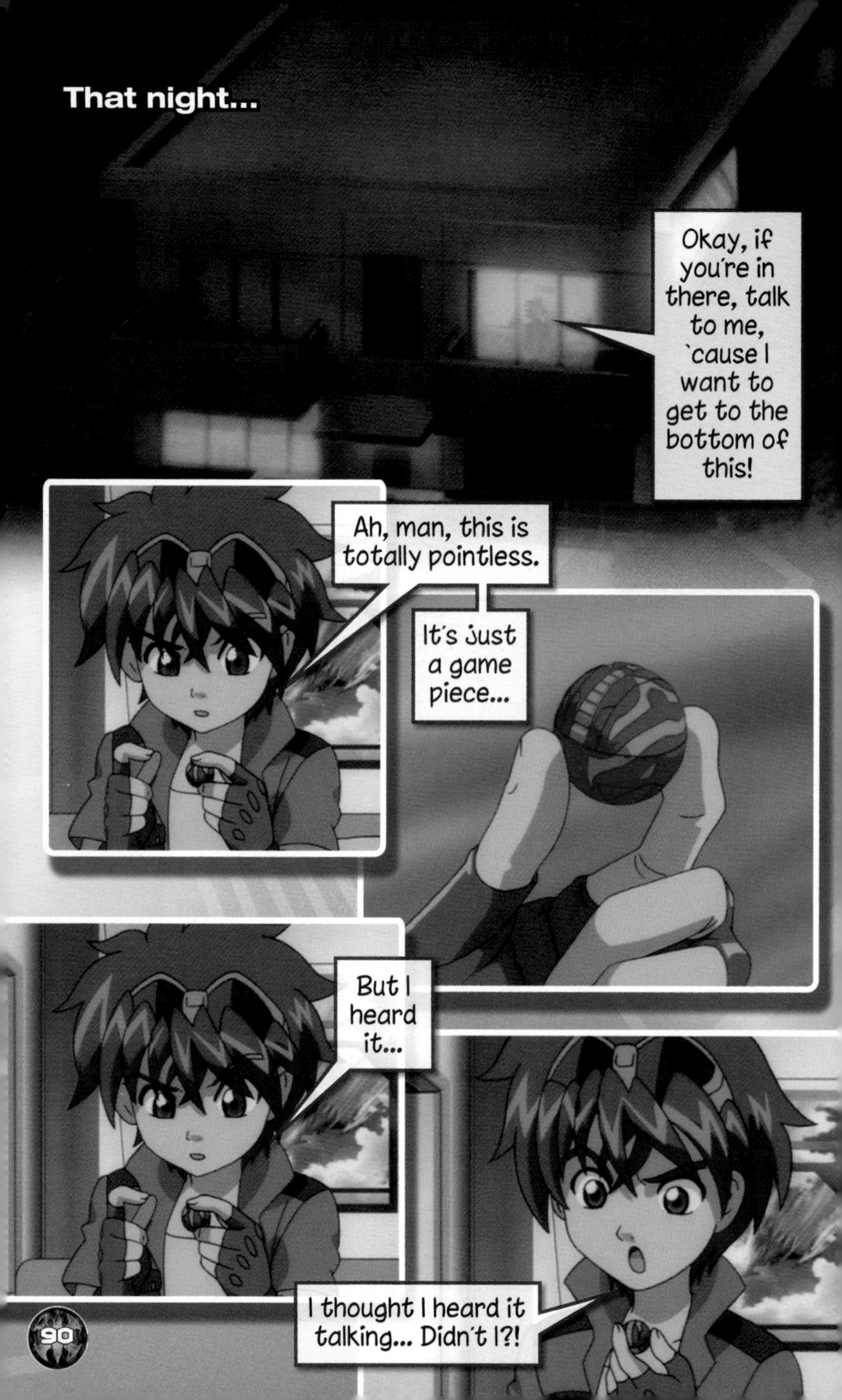
That night...
Okay, if you're in there, talk to me, `cause I want to get to the bottom of this!
Ah, man, this is totally pointless.
It's just a game piece...
But I heard it...
I thought I heard it talking... Didn't I?!

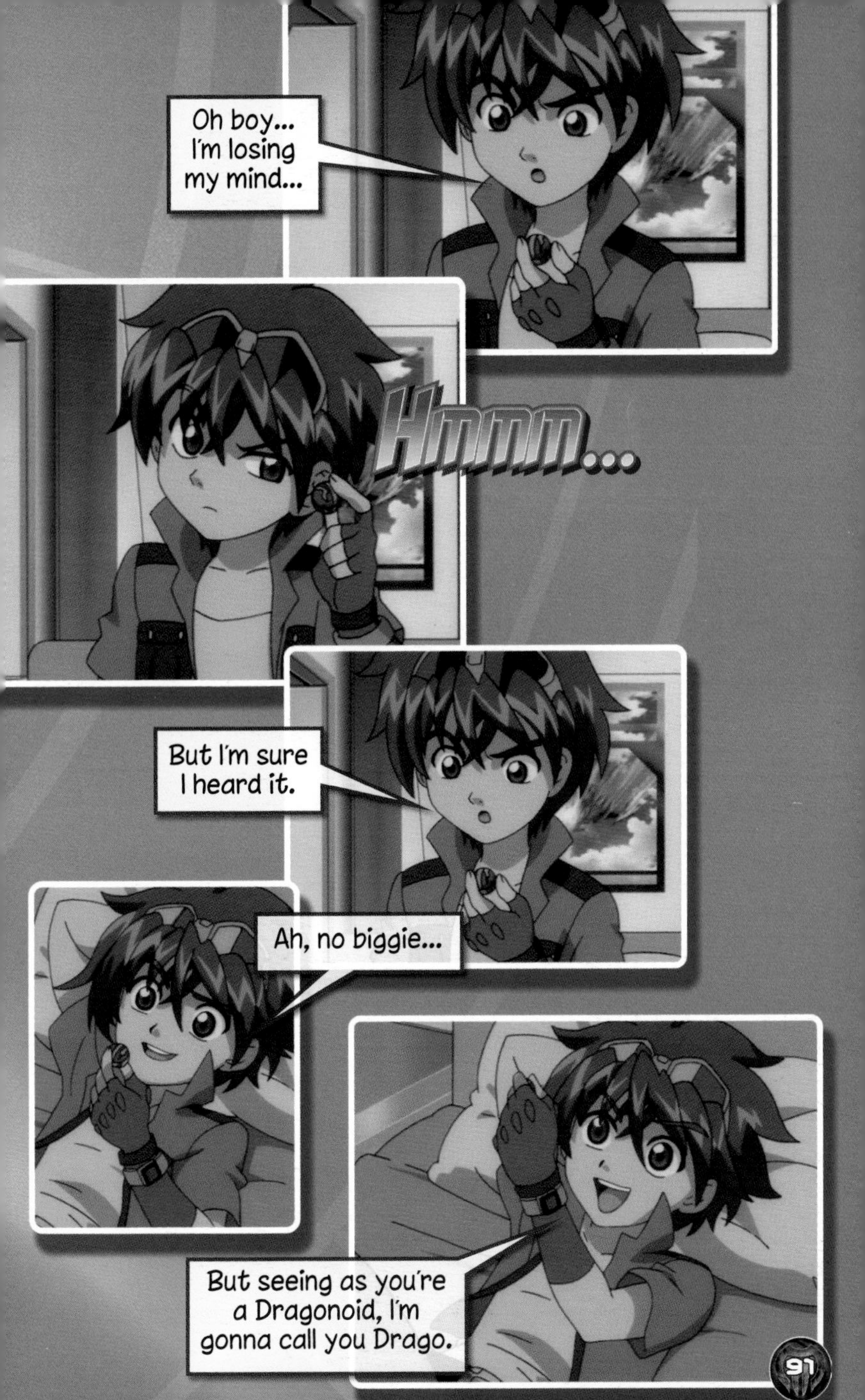

Oh boy... I'm losing my mind...
Hmmm...
But I'm sure I heard it.
Ah, no biggie...
But seeing as you're a Dragonoid, I'm gonna call you Drago.

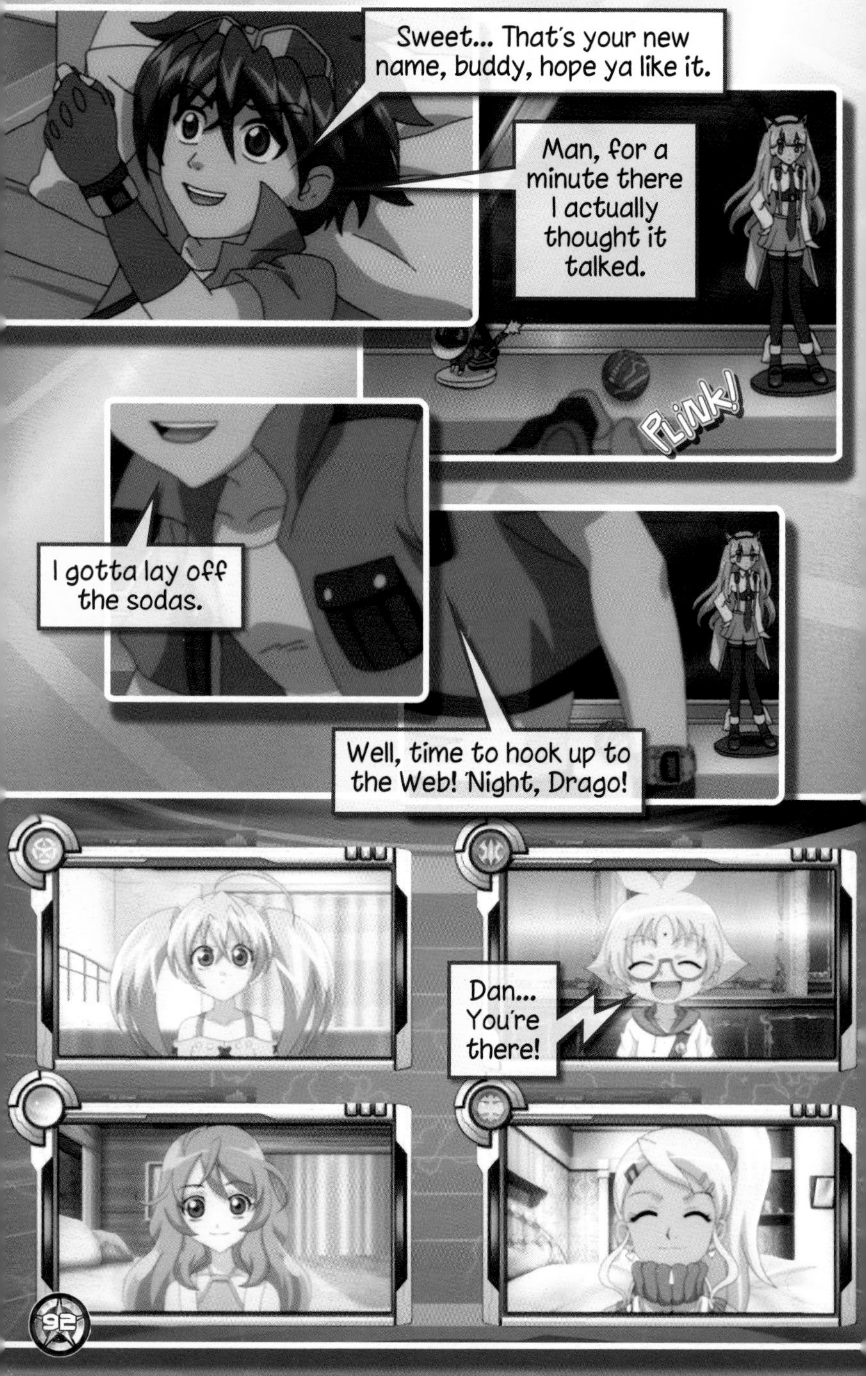

Sweet... That's your new name, buddy, hope ya like it.
Man, for a minute there I actually thought it talked.
PLINK!
I gotta lay off the sodas.
Well, time to hook up to the Web! Night, Drago!
Dan... You're there!

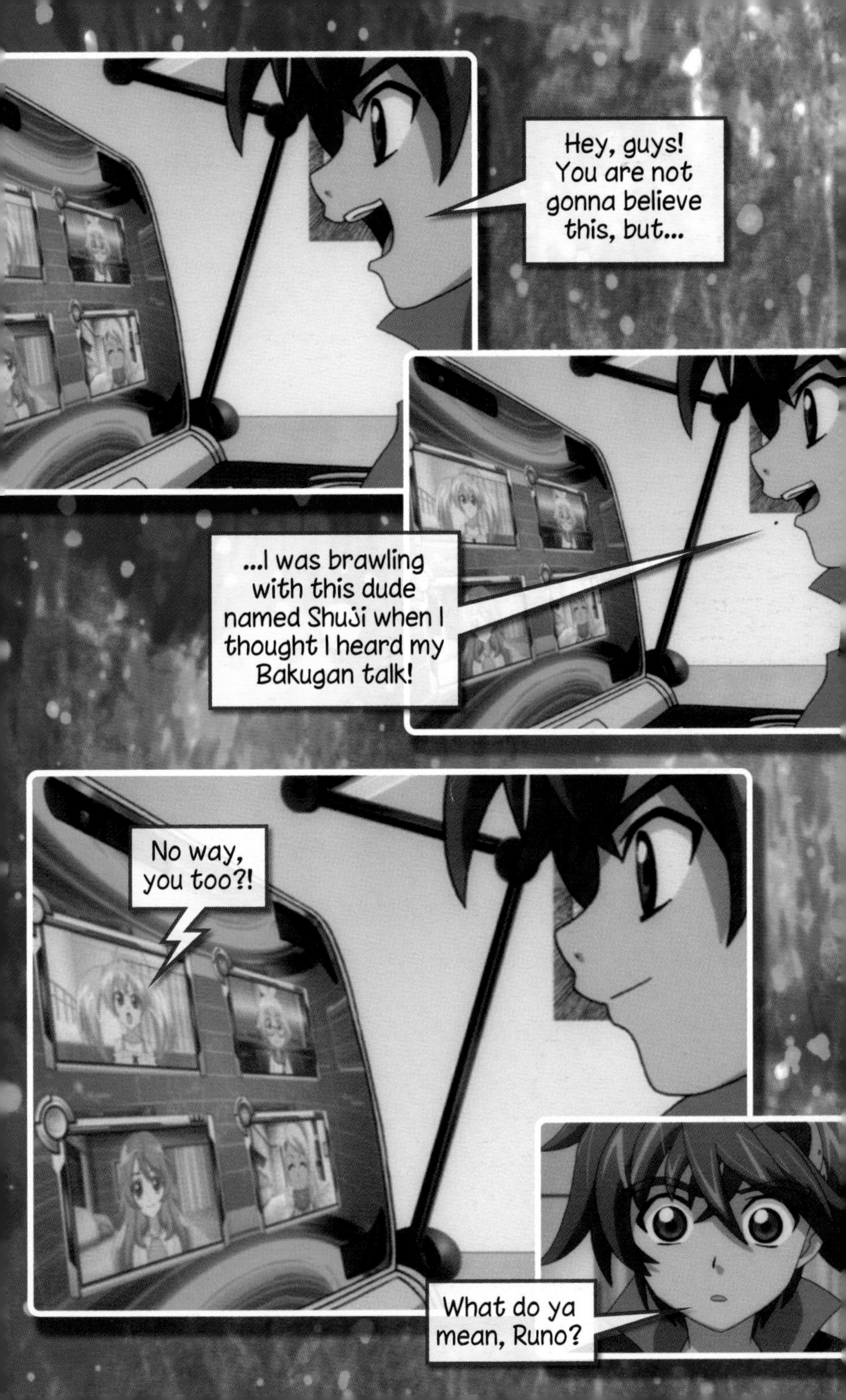
Hey, guys! You are not gonna believe this, but...
...I was brawling with this dude named Shuji when I thought I heard my Bakugan talk!
No way, you too?!
What do ya mean, Runo?

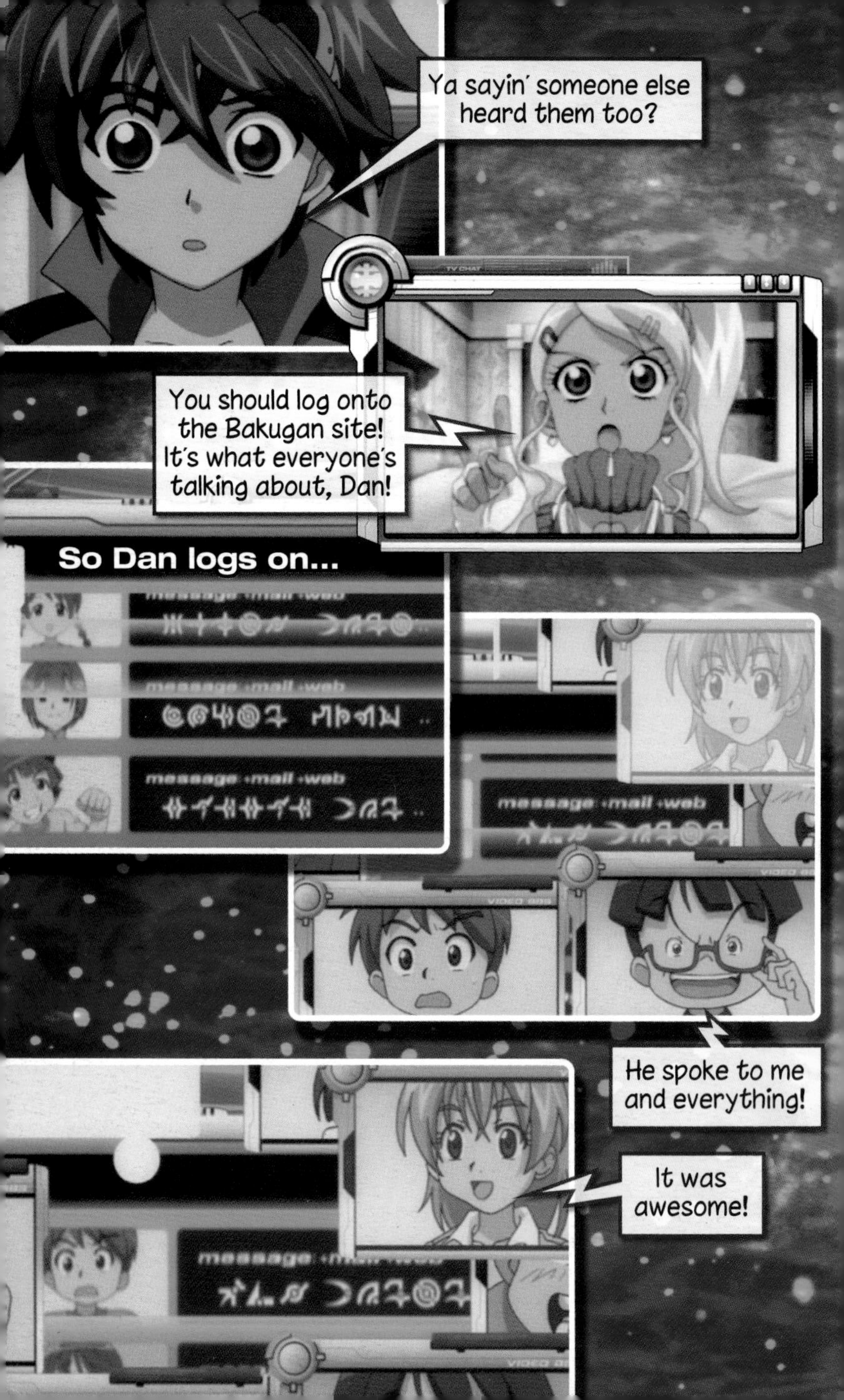
Ya sayin' someone else heard them too?
You should log onto the Bakugan site! It's what everyone's talking about, Dan!
So Dan logs on...
message·mail·web
message·mail·web
message·mail·web
message·mail·web
He spoke to me and everything!
It was awesome!
message

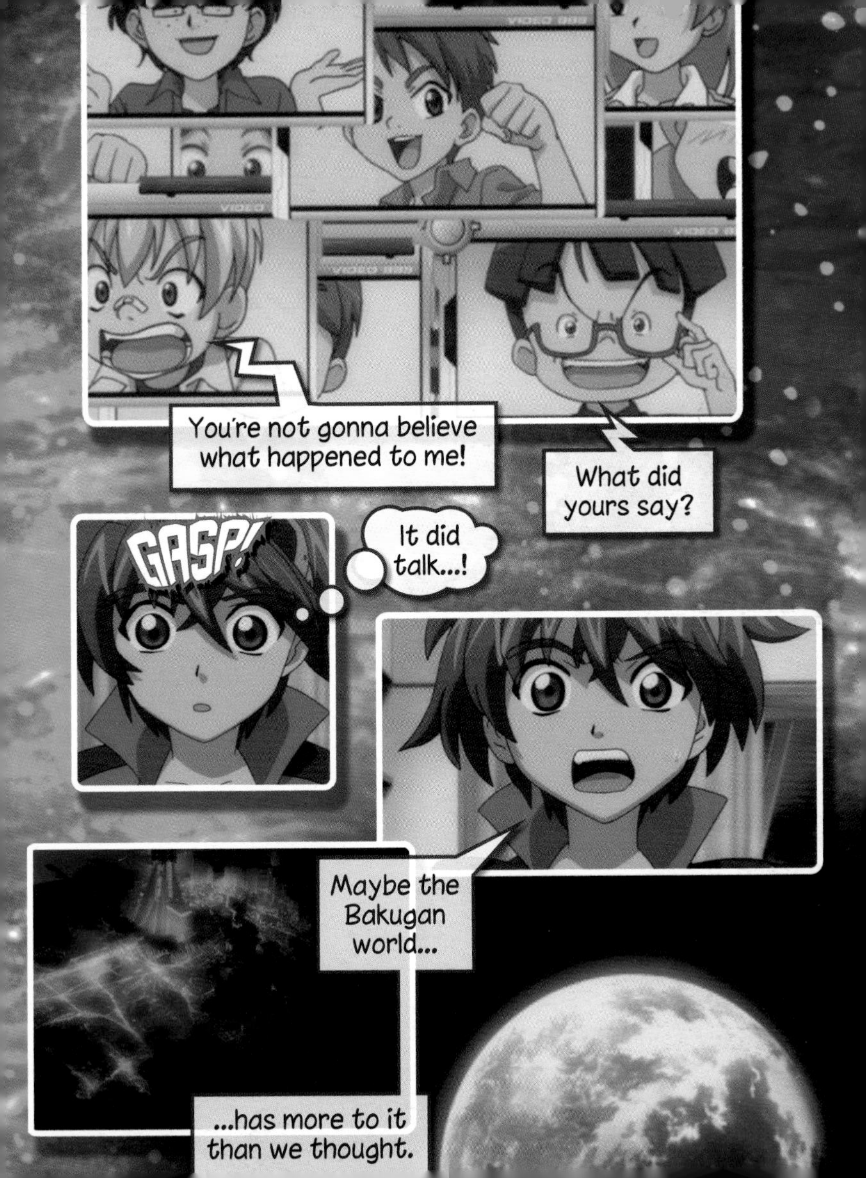

You're not gonna believe what happened to me!
What did yours say?
GASP!
It did talk...!
Maybe the Bakugan world...
...has more to it than we thought.

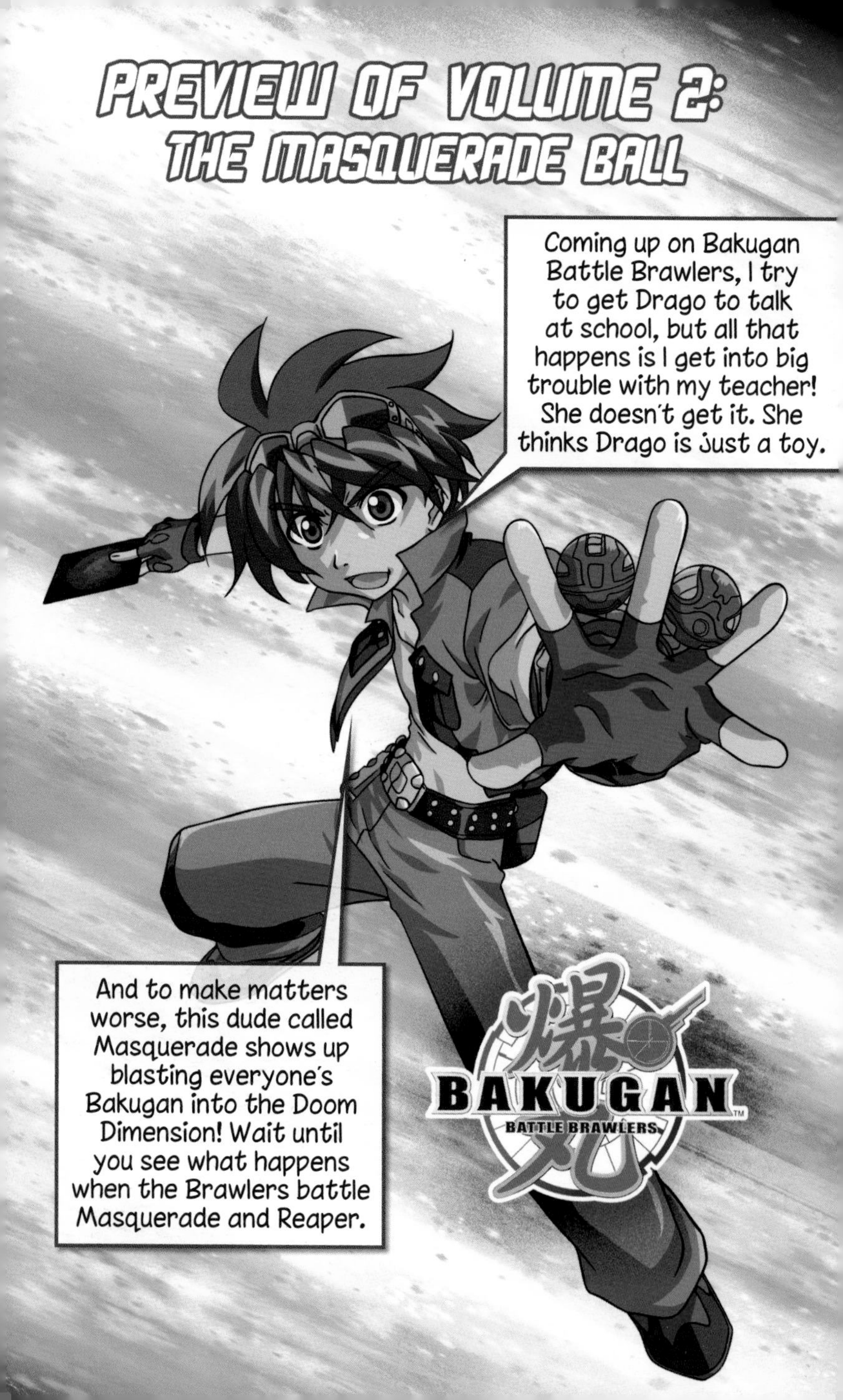
PREVIEW OF VOLUME 2:
THE MASQUERADE BALL
Coming up on Bakugan Battle Brawlers, I try to get Drago to talk at school, but all that happens is I get into big trouble with my teacher! She doesn't get it. She thinks Drago is just a toy.
And to make matters worse, this dude called Masquerade shows up blasting everyone's Bakugan into the Doom Dimension! Wait until you see what happens when the Brawlers battle Masquerade and Reaper.
BAKUGAN
BATTLE BRAWLERS